AMAZ[ ]
SECRETS
OF THE
BHAGAVAD
GITA

ED VISWANATHAN is the author of *Am I a Hindu?*, an international bestseller about Hindu culture that takes the form of a very lively discussion between a fourteen-year-old American-born Indian and his middle-aged father, covering every aspect of Hinduism in ninety chapters. *Am I a Hindu?* has been translated into Hindi (Rupa Publications) and Indonesian.

www.amazinggita.com
shrigita8@gmail.com

Praise for *Am I a Hindu?*

"This primer, serving some of the vast sweep of Hindu belief and practice, takes the form of dialog between a Hindu father and his American-born son. The son wants to understand his family's religious traditions and discover what is relevant for him today.

The book is useful not only to American Hindus but to those who want a nontechnical introduction to Hinduism as lived today. The book also explains how Hinduism engages in dialog with Western science and culture. Recommended for large public libraries and undergraduate collections."

Library Journal, USA

"The need of the hour not only for those overseas but even here in India."

The Hindu

"We treat this book as a very valuable contribution to the world of religions."

The Hindu Times, Nepal

"This book is extremely interesting to me, and I plan to share it with others who may be curious about Hindu religion."

Walter Isaacson, former Managing Editor,
Time magazine

AMAZING SECRETS OF THE BHAGAVAD GITA

ED VISWANATHAN

RUPA

Published by
Rupa Publications India Pvt. Ltd 2016
7/16, Ansari Road, Daryaganj
New Delhi 110002

Sales centres:
Allahabad Bengaluru Chennai
Hyderabad Jaipur Kathmandu
Kolkata Mumbai

ISBN: 978-81-291-4037-1

Second impression 2016

10 9 8 7 6 5 4 3 2

The moral right of the author has been asserted.

Printed at Rakmo Press Pvt. Ltd, New Delhi

Contents

Preface

After opening this book, the very first question that will arise in any reader's mind will be, *"Why do we need another book on the Bhagavad Gita?"*

Yes, it is true: we have several commentaries and interpretations of the Bhagavad Gita, translated into almost all of the languages in the world. So there is absolutely no point in putting out another translation of or commentary on the Bhagavad Gita, especially since many very prominent English translations and commentaries are available in the market by intellectuals like Dr S. Radhakrishnan, Mahatma Gandhi, Lokmanya Tilak, Eknath Easwaran, Maharishi Mahesh Yogi, Kashinath Trimbak Telang, Edwin Arnold, Christopher Isherwood, Franklin Edgerton, among others.

But I can assure you, this book is totally different. Instead of explaining each verse, chapter by chapter, this book gives a summary of the ideas and concepts found within the Bhagavad Gita, organized according to topic. Separate chapters deal with subjects such as salvation, selfless actions, creation and annihilation of the universe, the caste system, women, Sati, mind, sense organs, how to deal with stress, spirituality, the best time to pray, the best time to die.

Thus instead of going through all 700 verses to find the Bhagavad Gita's answers to your specific questions about a topic, you can just go through this book and get the answers.

In addition, instead of providing a "word for word" translation for every Sanskrit verse in the Gita, this book summarizes the meaning of each verse. In my experience, trying to understand "word for word" translations of the Sanskrit verses is cumbersome for readers.

The book also omits alternate names and references for characters and concepts (like Bhartata, Kauntaya, Partha, Parameswara, Rishikesha, Paranthapa, Mahabhahu, and so on). To me, all of these words are adjectives used by the authors to make the Bhagavad Gita look more attractive to readers. Even though the Bhagavad Gita is a dialog, in many chapters it appears to be a monologue by Lord Krishna. Instead, what we are actually seeing in the Gita is Lord Krishna explaining different systems of Hindu philosophy to educate his disciple, the warrior Arjuna, throughout all of the chapters. Therefore, this book just uses the names Lord Krishna and Arjuna in a much more straightforward manner.

I have to be honest with you: this book is aimed at people between the age of eighteen and thirty who normally do not have the time or patience to spend countless hours studying the Bhagavad Gita, but who would like to have a reference book to educate themselves and others about what the Bhagavad Gita has to say about many subjects.

On my part, I have read many prominent commentaries on the Gita before undertaking this Herculean task, so my book is also an aggregate of ideas from many prominent writers such as Dr S. Radhakrishnan, Sri Aurobindo, and Mahatma Gandhi. I thank all of those great writers and philosophers for enriching me with the necessary knowledge to write a book like this. I hope and pray that my humble book will help you in your search for truth.

October 26, 2015

Rishis (ancient Hindu seers) gave us all this knowledge (jnana) absolutely free and as such nobody has the right to profit from a book like this.

So after paying taxes and meeting all expenses associated with advertising and promoting this book, the rest of the proceeds from selling copies of this book will be donated to abused women's shelters and children's charities in India.

Chapter 1

Introduction

Grandson: Grandfather, I have read your book, Am I a Hindu?, in which you explained to my father—twenty-eight years ago, when he was a teenager—everything you knew about Hinduism and Hindu culture.

Today, I would like to know about the Bhagavad Gita. I am not interested in reading the entire Bhagavad Gita, but in how the Bhagavad Gita deals with the important aspects in a person's life.

Grandfather: First, thank you for your very kind words about my book! I never, ever thought it would become so popular when I wrote it a quarter century ago.

I really enjoyed your style of explaining Hinduism. In answering my father's questions, you quoted many great people from all over the world, and you brought forth positive ideas from other holy scriptures, such as the Bible, Dharmapada, and the Torah.

You are right. I never shied away from quoting Jesus Christ, or Lao Tzu, or Lord Buddha, or Socrates, or Plato, or Guru Nanak. I also did not shy away from expressing my displeasure at some of the negative things you see in Hinduism, such as the caste system in the past.

A few people were annoyed at me for quoting other religious scriptures. They felt that this was totally unnecessary. But those people forget the fact that *Am I a Hindu?* was written primarily for young people like your father and yourself, people who were born and brought up in the west, where they were bombarded by Christian evangelism. A child in an alien country, far away from India, is always subjected to all kinds of peer pressure and ridicule. It is the duty of every parent to teach their children all about their culture, and that's exactly why I wrote my last book.

But apart from that, we always have to search for truth, and we should never limit our search for truth only to what we find within Hinduism or the four corners of India.

> Rig Veda (1:89:1) states:
> "Aano bhadra krtavo yantu vishwatah."
> Let noble thoughts come to all from every direction.

The Hindu scriptures never state that we Hindus alone have all of the answers, or that we have the monopoly on God, or truth, or salvation. The great rishis (ancient Hindu seers) did not write, "Let noble thoughts come to us all from India." Instead, the rishis ask us to search for truth all over the universe.

But to return to the subject: it is so nice to know, my grandson, that you are interested in one of our most important scriptures—the Bhagavad Gita.

Once again, I am not interested in reading the entire Bhagavad Gita, but in how it deals with many important subjects.

I understand your point. There are thousands of translations of the Bhagavad Gita out there, and it does not make any sense for me to write another word for word translation.

Instead, I will give you, in simple sentences, as clear-cut a picture as I can of the essence of Lord Krishna's teachings. I will try to answer you as Lord Krishna would answer us if he were walking among us today.

Is the Bhagavad Gita our Holy Bible?

Unlike other religions, Hindus have no one book called the "Holy Bible of Hindus". We do not have just one holy scripture, but many. But many Hindus consider the Bhagavad Gita to be our most important scripture.

In the Sanskrit language (which the Bhagavad Gita is written in), Bhagavad means God, and Gita means song. Thus many describe the Bhagavad Gita as the "song of the God".

I like to call it "the roar of the God," since the Bhagavad Gita presents the teachings of God in the battlefield.

The Bhagavad Gita is the living word of God and is considered to be the most thought-provoking, powerful, life-giving, and enchanting book. Since everything discussed in the Bhagavad Gita is universal in nature, it should be read by everyone in the world.

The Bhagavad Gita systematically analyzes the problems we face in our daily lives, teaches us many ways to deal with those problems, and shows us many paths to attain self-realization.

There is no other scripture that can help every human being deal with his or her problems as well as the Bhagavad Gita can—whether or not he is a Hindu.

World Religions Chart

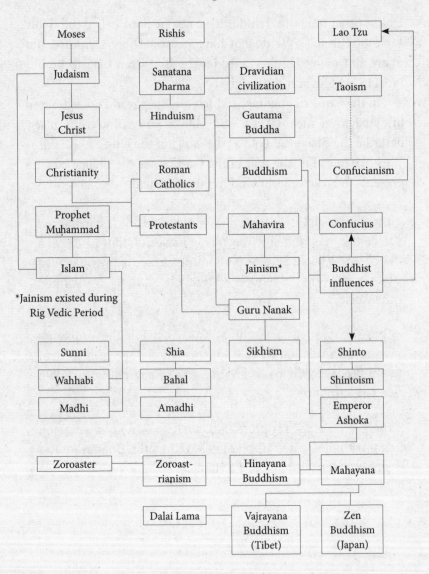

*Jainism existed during Rig Vedic Period

Hinduism in History

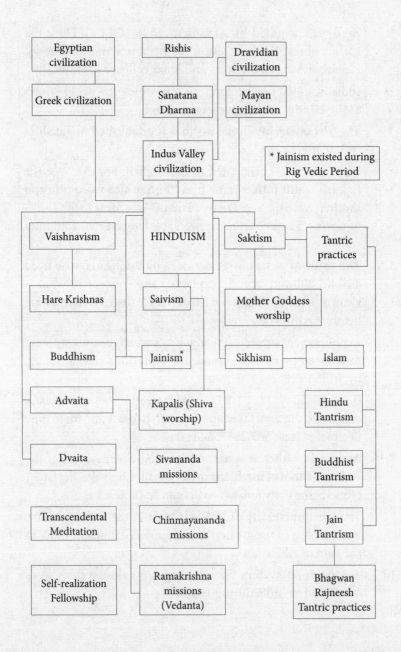

Ancient India's Contribution to the World

1.	Zero was invented by **Aryabhata** (476-550 CE). He is the author of several treatises on mathematics and astronomy. He also described the solar and lunar eclipses scientifically.
2.	India invented the **numeral system**, which the world knows as the **Hindu-Arabic numeral system**.
3.	The first university in the world was established in **Takshila** in 700 BCE.
4.	Many languages originated from **Sanskrit**. For example, the English words **father** came from the Sanskrit word **pita** and **mother**, from the Sanskrit word **mata**. According to the *Forbes* magazine, Sanskrit is the most suitable language for computer software.
5.	**The value of pi** was first calculated by Budhaana, who lived around 800 BCE and he explained the concept of what is known as the **Pythagorean theorem**. He discovered this long before Archimedes.
6.	Mathematical subjects like **algebra and trigonometry** were discovered by Indians. **Quadratic equations** were invented by Sridharacharya (1025 CE).
7.	Bhaskaracharya (1114–85 CE) in his treatise *Surya Siddhanta*, calculated the time taken for the earth to orbit the sun to nine decimal places (365.258756484 days).
8.	**Ayurveda**, which is a part of the Hindu Vedas, also is the **earliest school of medicine in the world**. Charvaka, the father of medicine consolidated Ayurveda 2,500 years ago.
9.	The great **university of Nalanda** built in the fourth century BCE was one of the greatest achievements of ancient India in the field of education.
10.	The **decimal system** as well as **place value system** were developed in India during 100 BCE.

Chapter 2

What is Hinduism?

Grandson: Before you start talking about the Bhagavad Gita, I want to know: is Hinduism a culture, or is it an organized religion like Christianity?

Grandfather: That is an excellent question. Hinduism is not an organized religion like Christianity or Islam. It has no founder. It has no Pope. It has no hierarchy. This is one reason why Hindus do not actively try to convert others to Hinduism unlike other religions.

Instead, Hinduism is the true culture of Indians in India. Many call it "a way of life". When you read the Hindu scriptures, you are actually studying the history and culture of India, just as in the first thirty-nine books of the Holy Bible, you are studying the culture and history of the Jews.

Hinduism and Judaism are the mothers of all modern religions in the world. Christianity and Islam came from Judaism, and still have close connections to it. The three religions all have Abraham as their common father figure, and they have many prophets in common. Similarly, Buddhism, Sikhism, and to some extent Jainism and Zoroastrianism came from Hinduism, and still have close connections to its culture. (Of course, Jainism existed during the Rig Vedic Period, when the Rig Veda was being written. Statues of Rishabha, the first Tirthankara and the founder of Jainism, were found in the Mohenjo-Daro and Harappa excavations.)

What was the original name of Hinduism?

Sanatana Dharma, or "righteousness forever", was the original name of Hinduism.

It was the Persians who came to India during the sixth century BCE who gave the name Hinduism to refer to the religion of the people living near the Indus river. In the Persian language, the letters *h* and *s* are pronounced almost the same, so they mistook the word Sindhu (the Sanskrit name for the Indus river) as Hindu.

What is the language in which the Hindu scriptures were written?

All the Hindu scriptures are written in Sanskrit, which is older than Hebrew and Latin.

The first words in the English language came from Sanskrit. According to the PBS documentary *The Story of English*, the word "mother" came from the Sanskrit word mata, and "father" came from the word pita.

Believe it or not, the word "geometry" came from the Sanskrit word gyaamiti, which means "measuring the earth". The word "trigonometry" came from the word trikonamiti, which means "measuring triangular forms".

Sanskrit, which literally means "cultured" or "refined", was the classical language of India, and it is the oldest and the most systematic language in the world. In 1987, a writer for *Forbes* said that Sanskrit was the mother of all the European languages and the most suitable language for computer software.

Who is a Hindu?

As far as I am concerned, anyone who searches after truth is automatically a Hindu, since Hinduism is man's relentless search after truth. According to that concept, a Jew, a Muslim, a Christian, a Buddhist, a Jain, a Sikh, or even an atheist who searches after truth is automatically a Hindu.

People used to say and write: *A Hindu is born and never converted.* Since Hinduism is a culture, a way of life, it did not make any sense even to talk about non-Hindus converting to Hinduism. But now, for the very first time, many are looking into the plight of a large number of people who love Hinduism and who really want to embrace Hindu culture. So now we allow those people who fall head over heels in love with Hinduism, such as actress Julia Roberts, to convert.

Under no circumstances do we ever force anyone to become a Hindu.

What attracts people to Hinduism?

The cardinal principle of Hinduism is the total freedom of thoughts and actions, and that is what attracts everyone to Hinduism. Hinduism never forbids anyone to question its fundamentals. Even an atheist has the right to condemn Hinduism in the public and still proudly proclaim that he or she is a Hindu.

Voltaire, in his essay on tolerance, wrote: "I may disagree with what you say, but I will defend to the death your right to say it." Hinduism is the embodiment of what Voltaire wrote.

In one part of Hinduism, you may come across people worshipping rats and other pests, and in another part, you will come across concepts that parallel quantum physics and the Bohr model of nuclear structure and reactions. Some Hindus discuss and promote the philosophy of Advaita ("There is only one") and others discuss and promote the philosophy of Dwaita ("duality").

Hindus have never ever killed or banished anyone from Hinduism for writing something contrary to the Vedas, for failing to observe a particular ritual, or for putting down the Hindu gods.

Eventually, everyone will embrace Hinduism (Sanatana Dharma) because Hinduism is man's everlasting search after truth. In the August 15, 2009 issue of *Newsweek*, its senior editor Lisa Miller wrote that we are all Hindus now. People may or may not actually convert to Hinduism. But they may embrace the Hindu concept of truths in their daily lives.

Everyone is attracted to Hinduism since

1) Hinduism allows the free flow of thoughts and actions.
2) There are no restrictions whatsoever in Hinduism. Everyone has the divine right to believe whatever he or she wants to believe and worship God in whatever form or under whatever name he or she wants.
3) There are no statements in Hindu scriptures starting with "Thou shalt not."
4) There are no statements saying that you have to be a Hindu to attain salvation.
5) There is no statement saying that Hinduism has a monopoly on God or the truth.
6) Nobody is thrown out of Hinduism.
7) Hindus accept everyone with open arms. When the Apostle Thomas (Doubting Thomas) landed in Cranganore during 52 CE, the people of Kerala greeted him with open arms.
8) Hindus have no problem worshipping in a Christian church or in a Jewish synagogue or in a Sikh gurudwara. Hindus believe in the Rig Veda's statement "Ekam Sat, Vipra Bahudha Vadanti." God is One, but theologians call God by many names.
9) A Hindu sees his or her personal God in all places of worship.
10) Even an atheist has the right to condemn Hinduism in public and still proudly proclaim himself or herself a Hindu.
11) Hindus firmly believe in the statement from the Mundaka Upanishad, "Satyameva Jayate"—Truth alone triumphs, not falsehood.

What attracts people to Hinduism?

The concept of utmost freedom of thoughts and actions.

Even atheists have the freedom to condemn Hinduism in public and still proudly say they are Hindus.

Who is the founder of Hinduism?

Hinduism, known as **Sanatana Dharma**, (righteousness forever) is not an organized religion like Islam or Christianity.

As such Hinduism does not have any founder.

It is the research output of countless learned men called rishis, the ancient saints of India throughout thousands of years.

There is no word Hindu or Hinduism in any of the Hindu scriptures.

What is the original name of Hinduism?

Sanatana Dharma or "righteousness forever" was the original name of Hinduism. It was the Persians who came to India during the sixth century BCE who began using the name "Hinduism" to refer to the religion of the people living near the Indus river.

In the Persian language, the letters *h* and *s* are pronounced almost the same, so they mistook the word Sindhu (the Sanskrit name for the Indus river) to be Hindu.

There is no word Hindu or Hinduism in any of the Hindu scriptures.

Hinduism is a culture,
a way of life.

It is not an
organized religion like
Islam or Christianity.

That is the reason Hindus do not try to convert
others to their religion or profess a monopoly on
God or truth, as other faiths do.

The Hindu rishis were
actually scientists of
the ancient age.

This is the reason why they allowed
all types of ideas, including an
atheistic philosophy, to flourish.

This is also the reason why they
never professed to have a
monopoly on truth,
God, or salvation.

Not even one Hindu has been banished
or killed because he or she preached
against the Vedas or made fun of God.

Chapter 3

What are the Hindu scriptures?

Grandson: You mentioned that there are hundreds of scriptures in Hinduism. What are they?

Grandfather: Excellent question. According to Hindu scriptures, knowledge (jnana) always existed in the form of sounds in the universe. Thus jnana started as shruti—that which is heard.

The rishis of ancient times, once they had perfected themselves, heard eternal truths. They taught those truths to their disciples by telepathy, and later disciples wrote them in books.

Hindu scriptures are divided into two parts.

Shruti	"That which is heard"	Vedas and Upanishads
Smriti	"That which is remembered"	Rest of the scriptures

What are the Vedas?

The Vedas claim to teach men the highest aspects of the truths which can lead them to God. The word Veda came from the root word *vid*, meaning "to know". The Vedas are Shruti scriptures, and they are considered apaurusheya (not human): in other words, it is believed that God wrote the Vedas.

The Vedas state that self-realization is the one and only goal of a human life. They also describe the rituals and ceremonies necessary to attain self-realization.

The four Vedas are as follows:

Rig Veda	Knowledge of hymns	10,589 verses
Yajur Veda	Knowledge of liturgy	3,988 verses
Sama Veda	Knowledge of music	1,549 verses
Atharva Veda	Knowledge given by Sage Atharvan	6,000 verses

There is no mention of the Atharva Veda in the Gita. The Bhagavad Gita only mentions the first three Vedas: Rig Veda, Yajur Veda, and Sama Veda.

Within the Vedas, there are four kinds of texts:

Samhitas	Basic texts for hymns to deities, formulas, and chants. The Sanskrit word samhita means "put together".
Brahmanas	Description of rituals, as well as the directions for performing them. The word originated from the word Brahmin. Brahmins are the original Hindu priests, and they follow the Brahmanas to conduct rituals.
Aranyakas	Contain mantras and interpretations of rituals. These writings are also known as the "forest books," since they are used by saints who meditate in the forests.
Upanishads	Texts revealing ultimate truths by different saints. The Upanishads teach men that there is only one God, Brahman, and that every one of us is part of the immortal soul, Atman, which is also Brahman.

What are the Upanishads?

The Upanishads are the brains of Hindu culture. Niels Bohr, the great Danish physicist who made foundational contributions to understanding atomic structure and quantum theory, said: "When I have doubts, I go into the Upanishads to ask questions."

The word Upanishad comes from the combination of three words: upa (near), ni (down), and shad (sit). When the teachings of the Upanishads were conveyed from masters to students, the students sat very close to the masters so that nobody could overhear the teachings.

There are a total of 108 Upanishads. Thirteen of them are considered the most important. They are:

1) Isha Upanishad
2) Kena Upanishad
3) Katha Upanishad
4) Prashna Upanishad
5) Mundaka Upanishad
6) Mandukya Upanishad
7) Aitareya Upanishad
8) Taittiriya Upanishad
9) Chandogya Upanishad
10) Brihadaranyaka Upanishad
11) Kaushitaki Upanishad
12) Shvetashvatara Upanishad
13) Maitri Upanishad

What are the Upavedas?

In Sanskrit, Upaveda means "applied knowledge". There are four Upavedas.

Ayurveda	Hindu science of health and longevity consisting of more than 100,000 verses. Still, it is considered to be an Upaveda of the Atharva Veda.
Dhanur Veda	Hindu science of archery and war
Gandharva Veda	Hindu science of music
Arthashastra	Written by the scholar Chanakya (or Kautilya), this is an ancient Indian treatise on political science, statecraft, economic policy, and military strategy for kings.

What are the Vedangas?

The Vedangas are scriptures attached to the Vedas.

Dharma Sutras	The most important of these scriptures are the sutras written by Apastamba, Gautama, Baudhayana, and Vasistha.
Dharma Shastras	These comprise Manu Smriti, Yajnavalkya Smriti, Narada Smriti, Visnu Smriti, Brihaspati Smriti, and Katyayana Smriti.
Jyotisha	Traditional Hindu system of astrology
Kalpa	Rituals and legal matters
Shiksha	Phonetics
Chandas	Poetic meter
Nirukta	Interpretation of the origins of words

What are the Darshanas?

The Darshanas are the six philosophical systems, or schools of thought. Each of these six philosophies explains the unwritten laws of the universe in its own special way. The ultimate goal of these philosophies is to eradicate ignorance, so that people can finally attain salvation.

The six philosophies are as follows:

Sankhya	Founded by Sage Kapila. Proposes that the two ultimate realities are Purusha (spirit) and Prakriti (matter). This philosophy is somewhat atheistic in nature since no God is mentioned anywhere within it. The Bhagavad Gita starts with this philosophy. Lord Krishna says that Sankhya and Yoga are essentially the same. In the Bhagavad Gita, Lord Krishna said: "Among siddhas (perfected beings), I am Sage Kapila." (10:26)
Yoga	Raja Yoga and Hatha Yoga. Very close to Sankhya in many aspects.

Nyaya	Logically proves the existence of God based on the Vedas.
Vaisheshika	Proposes that all objects in the physical universe are made of indivisible paramanu (atom).
Mimamsa	The meaning of Mimamsa in Sanskrit is "investigation".
Vedanta	Means the "end of Veda". Vedanta philosophy is further divided into two schools—Advaita (only one) and Dwaita (two). Vedanta is mentioned in the Bhagavad Gita in verses 13:5 and 18:12.

What are the Ithihasas?

The word ithihas means "historical event" or "so indeed it was". Hindus have two epics, or Ithihasas. They are:

| Ramayana | A Sanskrit epic poem about Lord Rama written by the Hindu sage Valmiki. It has seven chapters and 24,000 verses. |
| Mahabharata | An epic poem written by Rishi Veda Vyasa. It has nineteen chapters and 220,000 verses. |

The Mahabharata is the longest poem in the world.

What are the Puranas?

The word purana means ancient. The Puranas are ancient scriptures in verse, usually dedicated to specific deities. There are eighteen very important Puranas. The most important is the Srimad Bhagavatam, addressed to Lord Vishnu.

The other seventeen important Puranas are as follows: Agni Purana, Bhavishya Purana, Brahma Purana, Brahmanda Purana, Brahmavaivarta Purana, Garuda Purana, Harivamsa Purana, Kurma Purana, Linga Purana, Markandeya Purana, Matsya Purana, Narada Purana, Padma Purana, Skanda Purana, Shiva Purana, Vamana Purana, Varaha Purana, Vayu Purana, and Vishnu Purana.

Apart from these, Hinduism also includes many minor Puranas.

What are the Agamas?

The Agamas are sectarian scriptures that discuss the doctrines associated with certain deities, as well as the arrangement of their temples.

Vaishnava Agamas	Lord Vishnu
Saiva Agamas	Lord Shiva
Sakta Agamas	Mother Goddess Shakti

What are the Tantras?

The word tantra is made up of the two Sanskrit words: tanoti (expansion) and trayati (liberation). The word refers to the liberation of energy and expansion of consciousness from its gross form.

The Tantras contain methods to expand the mind and liberate its dormant potential energy. Tantric principles form the basis of all yogic practices, and many concepts in Hinduism, including mandalas, chakras, kundalini, mudras, and yantra, originally come from the Tantras. The Tantras also delve deep into human sexuality.

Historically, the Tantras were associated with the worship of the Mother Goddess, Shakti. The twentieth-century guru Bhagwan Shree Rajneesh, later known as "Osho", was an advocate of the Tantras.

Do all Hindu philosophies include the belief in God?

Amazing as it may sound, Hinduism—unlike all other religions in the world—includes nastika (heretical) philosophies such as Charvaka, which did not accept the authority of the Vedas and which believed in materialism. This philosophy rejected many aspects of the Hindu faith, including the belief in God, samsara, karma, afterlife, and reincarnation. The Charvaka tradition ceased to exit after the twelfth century.

Beyond that which we've discussed above, there are still a lot more scriptures in Hinduism. I should say that there are more than a thousand scriptures in Hinduism!

Charvaka Atheistic Philosophy

While other religions burn and kill people for disagreeing with what the religious hierarchy taught, Hinduism allows and supports an atheistic philosophy.

The Charvaka atheistic philosophy rejects the existence of God and considers religion as an aberration.

The Charvaka atheistic philosophy preached:

1.	All things are made of earth, air, fire, and water.
2.	That which cannot be perceived does not exist; to exist implies to be perceivable.
3.	Heaven and hell are nothing but human inventions. The only goal of human beings is to enjoy pleasures and avoid pain.
4.	The Vedas are written by buffoons.

Hindu Scriptures

Shruti	That which is heard	Vedas and Upanishads
Smriti	That which is remembered	Rest of the scriptures

Shruti Scriptures

1	Vedas	Rig Veda Sam Veda Yajur Veda Atharva Veda
2	Upanishads	108 Upanishads—thirteen are very important.
3	Brahmanas	These include commentaries, explanation of proper methods, and meaning of Vedic Samhita rituals in the four Vedas.
4	Aranyakas	They include rituals, discussion of rituals, as well as philosophical speculations.

Smriti Scriptures

1	Vedangas	Dharma Sutras (Manu Smriti, Gautama Smriti, Yatnyavalkya Smriti)
2	Darsanas	Hindu philosophies—Mimamsa, Sankhya, Vaisheshika, Yoga, Nyaya, Vedanta (Advaita and Dvaita.
3	Ithihasas	Ramayana Mahabharata (Bhagavad Gita).
4	Puranas	Eighteen are most important.
5	Upavedas	Ayurveda, Dhanurveda, Gandharva Veda, Artha Shastra
6	Agamas	Vaishnava Agamas, Saiva Agamas, Sakti Agamas
7	Upangas	Logical and ritual forms of thoughts
8	Tantras	Very complex non-Vedic teachings. Mantras and many other elements in Hinduism came from the Tantras.
9	Charvaka	Atheistic philosophy

Chapter 4

What is the Bhagavad Gita?

Grandson: What is the Bhagavad Gita?

Grandfather: The Bhagavad Gita tells the story of a very lively conversation between the warrior prince, Arjuna, and Lord Krishna about every aspect of life. It takes place prior to the outbreak of the Mahabharata War, which was fought between two families, the Pandavas and the Kauravas, on the battlefield of Kurukshethra.

The word Kurukshethra comes from the Kuru Dynasty, founded by the great King Kuru. Kurukshethra consists of two words, Kuru—Kuru Dynasty—and Kshetra—region or place. Thus Kurukshethra means "the region of the Kuru Dynasty".

Amazing! Please explain to me more about the Bhagavad Gita.

The Bhagavad Gita is described as the "essence of the Vedas".

In a nine-verse poem often attached to the Bhagavad Gita called "Gita Dhyanam" (the Invocation to the Gita), it is written:
"If all Upanishads can be considered as cows;
Then the Bhagavad Gita can be considered as milk."

The "Gita Dhyanam" is not a part of the main Bhagavad Gita, but it is commonly published along with the Bhagavad Gita as a prefix. According to Swami Chinmayananda, "Gita Dhyanam" was written by the Indian philosopher Madhusudana Sarasvati (1540–1640).

The Bhagavad Gita is essentially a "question and answer" dialog about every aspect of life, between the *first person*, Lord Krishna, and the *second person*, warrior prince Arjuna. The dialog is seen and heard telepathically by the *third person*, the advisor and charioteer Sanjaya, who narrates the story to the *fourth person*, the blind King Dhritarashtra.

Some compare the Bhagavad Gita to the *Sermon on the Mount* and the Buddhist *Dhammapada*. But unlike these scriptures, the Gita is written in a question and answer format, and it deals with its subject matter in a different way.

Chapter 5

Where does the Bhagavad Gita appear in the Hindu scriptures?

Grandson: Where does the Bhagavad Gita appear in the Hindu scriptures?

Grandfather: The Bhagavad Gita appears in the Bhishma Parva (literally, the chapter of Bhishma) of the great epic the Mahabharata.

What is the Mahabharata?

Hindus have two epics, called the Ithihasas. The two epics are the Ramayana and Mahabharata. The Ramayana is the story of Lord Rama, written by Sage Valmiki. It is the story of Lord Rama and Princess Sita. Lord Rama is one of the avatars of Lord Vishnu, and the Ramayana projects Hindu ideals of life.

Sage Valmiki wrote the whole Ramayana as the narration of a crying dove who just lost her lover to a hunter's wicked arrow. This beautiful poem consists of 24,000 verses.

There are many versions of the Ramayana. The Hindi version was written by Sage Tulsidas. The Malayalam version (the language of the Indian state of Kerala) was written by Tuncattu Eluttacchan. The original text was written in very stylish Sanskrit language.

The Mahabharata tells the story of the war between the

Pandavas and Kauravas. It is 220,000 verses long, divided into eighteen Parvas, or chapters. It is lengthier than Homer's *Odyssey*, and it consists of episodes, dialogs, stories, discourses, and sermons. The Bhagavad Gita is part of this epic.

Chapter 6

Who wrote the Mahabharata?

Grandson: Who wrote the Mahabharata?

Grandfather: It was written by Rishi Veda Vyasa with the help of Lord Ganesha. According to legend, Sage Narada insisted that Rishi Veda Vyasa, who had already written many wonderful books, should also write the Mahabharata in order to help the common man understand the subtle truths of the universe.

So Rishi Veda Vyasa sought the help of Lord Ganesha, asking the god to write down what Veda Vyasa was saying.

Lord Ganesha told him: "The moment you stop reciting, I will stop writing forever."

Veda Vyasa replied: "Okay, I agree to your terms—provided that you fully understand the meaning of everything I say before you write."

Both agreed, and together they wrote the great epic, the Mahabharata.

Who was Veda Vyasa?

He was the son of Rishi Parasara and the fisherwoman Satyavati. In his youth, he was called Krishna Dvaipayana: he was born on the island of Dvipa, hence Dvaipayana, and his skin was black in color, hence Krishna. Since he did penance at Badri, he was also known as Baadaraayana.

In Sanskrit, vyasa means to differentiate or split. Krishna Dvaipayana was the person who first divided the Vedas into their current four-part classification, so he became known as Veda Vyasa, or "Splitter of the Vedas".

Rishi Veda Vyasa is also the author of the Brahma Sutras, and many consider him to be the author of the eighteen major Puranas, including the Srimad Bhagavatam. He was a proponent of the Advaita philosophy.

So what does rishi mean? You always address Veda Vyasa as Rishi Veda Vyasa.

That is a very good observation. I am very proud of you. The word rishi came from the Sanskrit root word *rsh*, meaning "to go, to move". So a rishi is someone who makes things happen in society.

All Hindu seers during Vedic period such as Veda Vyasa, Vishvamitra, Vamadeva, Atri, Bharadvaja, Vasistha, Angiras, Kanva are called rishis. Similarly, all female Hindu seers at the time such as Lopamudra, Apala, Kadru, Visvavara, Ghosha, Juhu, Vagambhrini, Paulomi, Yami, Indrani, Savitri, and Devayani are called Rshikäs.

Chapter 7

How many chapters are in the Mahabharata?

Grandson: How many chapters are in the Mahabharata?

Grandfather: The Mahabharata originally had eighteen chapters, or parvas. Over time, an additional chapter, the Harivamsa Parva, was added, bringing the total to nineteen parvas.

1	Adi Parva	This chapter is known as the "Book of the Beginning". It introduces all of the characters, including their births and lineage.
2	Sabha Parva	This chapter is known as the "Book of the Assembly Hall". It shows a game of dice between the Pandavas and the Kauravas, and ends with the exile of the Pandavas to the forest.
3	Vana Parva	This chapter is known as the "Book of Forest Life". It presents the adventures of the Pandavas in the forest.
4	Virata Parva	This chapter is known as the "Book of Virata". It tells the story of the Pandavas during their time living with King Virata in their thirteenth year of exile.
5	Udyoga Parva	In this chapter, Lord Krishna tries to avoid a war between the Pandavas and the Kauravas. Lord Krishna's effort fails, and war is declared.

6	Bhishma Parva	This chapter is known as the "Book of Bhishma". The Mahabharata War begins. This chapter tells the story of the first ten days, when Bhishma was the commander of the Kaurava army. *The Bhagavad Gita appears in this chapter.*
7	Drona Parva	This chapter is known as the "Book of Drona". It tells of the next five days of the war, during which Drona was the commander of the Kaurava army.
8	Karna Parva	This chapter is known as the "Book of Karna". It tells of the next two days of the war, during which Karna was the commander of the Kaurava army.
9	Salya Parva	This chapter is known as the "Book of Salya". It tells of the single day during which Salya was the commander of the Kaurava army. In this chapter, the Kaurava Duryodhana is brutally killed by the Pandava brother, Bhima. After that, the war ends.
10	Sauptika Parva	In this chapter, Ashwatthaman (son of the late Drona) does the unthinkable: he attacks and kills the Pandava Panchali's sons at night in total darkness. He also tries to kill the unborn son of Abhimanyu (King Parikshit). Lord Krishna prevents his attempt and curses Ashwatthaman
11	Stree Parva	In this chapter, the Pandavas meet with King Dhritarashtra after battle and take over the kingdom. Yudhisthira becomes the king.
12	Shanti Parva	In this chapter, Bhishma finally leaves his body.
13	Anusasana Parva	In this chapter, after Bhishma's departure from earth, grief-stricken Yudhisthira and the rest of the Pandavas return home.
14	Aswamedhika Parva	This chapter narrates the royal ceremony of Aswamedhika conducted by Yudhisthira.

15	Asramavasika Parva	In this chapter, King Dhritarashtra retires into the woods and dies after three years.
16	Mausala Parva	In this chapter, Lord Krishna leaves the earth, and his Yadava clan is destroyed thirty-six years after the battle.
17	Mahaprasthanika Parva	In this chapter, the Pandavas go on a pilgrimage and die one after another, including Panchali.
18	Svargarohana Parva	In this chapter, Yudhisthira goes to heaven on Devandra's chariot. He also visits hell in this chapter.
19	Harivamsa Parva	This chapter describes the creation of the cosmos and the history of the kings of the Solar and Lunar dynasties, leading up to the birth of Lord Krishna.

When was the Bhagavad Gita written?

It is very difficult to state the exact time period. Many assume it was written thousands of years before the birth of Jesus Christ. We do not know the exact date. The Bhagavad Gita might even have been written by many brilliant minds over a period of centuries.

Chapter 8

What is the story of the Mahabharata?

Grandson: What is the story of the Mahabharata?

Grandfather: It is very difficult to narrate the story of the Mahabharata in a few words. Anyway, let me try to narrate to you in brief.

Lord Brahma was born out of the navel of Lord Vishnu. This begins the lineage:

Atri	The son of Lord Brahma.
Soma	The son of Atri.
Buddha and Pururavas	The sons of Soma.
Ayus	The son of Pururavas.
Yayathi, Dushyantha, Itharata, Kuru, and Santhanu	Born in the lineage of Ayus. Eventually, Santhanu becomes the king of the Kauravas.
Bhishma (also known as Gangeya, or Devavrata)	The son of King Santhanu and Mother Ganges.
Chitrangada and Vichitravirya	The sons of King Santhanu and Satyavati (the fisherwoman).

After the birth of Bhishma, Mother Ganges separated from King Santhanu. Santhanu, on his part, fell in love with a fisherwoman named Satyavati. In return for his daughter's hand in marriage to Santhanu, Satyavati's father made Bhishma take a vow of celibacy throughout his life.

Through Satyavati, Santhanu had two children named Chitrangada and Vichitravirya. They married two daughters of the king of Kasi, Ambika and Ambalika.

However, Chitrangada was killed by a Gandharva (a celestial being), and Vichitravirya died of an illness. Suddenly the country was left without a ruler. So Queen Satyavati summoned her son, Rishi Veda Vyasa, to impregnate both the princesses. Rishi Veda Vyasa impregnated them, as well as a servant girl.

Princess Ambika gave birth to	Dhritarashtra
Princess Ambalika gave birth to	Pandu
The servant girl gave birth to	Vidura

As Dhritarashtra was blind, Pandu, though the younger prince, became the king. He married two princesses, Kunti and Madri. Kunti gave birth to three sons named Yudhisthira (also known as Dharmaputra), Bhima, and Arjuna. Madri gave birth to two sons, Nakula and Sahadeva.

All five children of Pandu were collectively called the Pandavas.

Who were the Pandavas?	
Yudhisthira (also known as Dharmaputra), Bhima, and Arjuna	Sons of King Pandu and Kunti. Kunti also had a son before marriage whose name was Karna.
Nakula and Sahadeva	Sons of King Pandu and Madri.

Dhritarashtra married Princess Gandhari and had one hundred sons and one daughter. The eldest son's name was Duryodhana, and the daughter's name was Dussala. These children were called the Kauravas.

Who were the Kauravas?	
Duryodhana and his ninety-nine brothers	Sons of King Dhritarashtra and Gandhari.
Dussala	Only daughter of King Dhritarashtra and Gandhari.

King Pandu met with an accidental death, so Dhritarashtra was crowned as the king. But he was totally under the influence of Duryodhana, and couldn't rule.

When the Pandavas came to stay in Hastinapura, the capital city, Duryodhana tried to kill them in many ways. This family feud between the Kauravas and the Pandavas finally resulted in a fierce battle known as the Mahabharata War.

Lord Krishna sided with the Pandavas in the war. All the Kauravas were killed, and Yudhisthira became the king after the war. Some years later Lord Krishna—along with his clansmen, the Yadavas—left this world. Immediately after that, Yudhisthira and his brothers, along with their wife Panchali, handed over the kingdom to Parikshit, Arjuna's grandson, and left for heaven.

This is the story of the epic, the Mahabharata.

Who's who of Mahabharata?

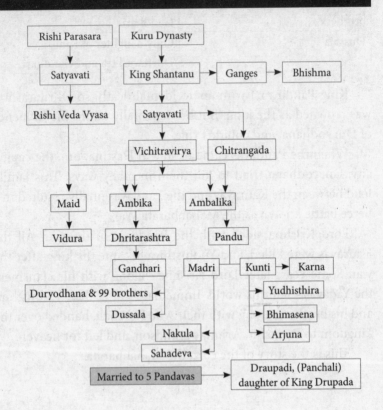

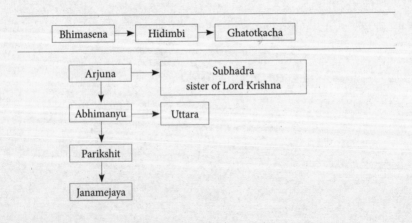

Chapter 9

What is the story of the Bhagavad Gita?

Grandson: What is the story of the Bhagavad Gita?

Grandfather: The Bhagavad Gita takes the form of a conversation between the warrior prince Arjuna and his charioteer and friend Lord Krishna at the outset of the Mahabharata War.

Just before the beginning of the war, Arjuna realized that he would have to kill all of his kinsmen as well as his teachers, and he refused to fight. Lord Krishna, trying to convince him to join the battle, advised him in detail on a variety of subjects throughout the 700 verses of the Bhagavad Gita. At the end, Arjuna took Lord Krishna's advice and fought a very fierce war.

The Bhagavad Gita's 700 verses are divided into eighteen chapters. It deals in depth with all four yogas, or ways to attain God-realization.

There are many versions of the Bhagavad Gita available in the market. The very first English translation of the Bhagavad Gita was written by Sir Charles Wilkins in 1785, with an introduction by Warren Hastings, the first Governor General of India. But the most popular English translation was written by Sir Edwin Arnold, under the title *The Song Celestial*.

The Bhagavad Gita has an answer to every problem a man or a woman may face in his or her life. It never commands us about what to do. Instead, it gives us the pros and cons of every issue, and the final decision is left to us.

Throughout the Bhagavad Gita, you will not come across even one line starting with "Thou shalt not".

The Bhagavad Gita asserts, "salvation is for everybody." The only difference between people is the time salvation will take. The best among us will attain it within one lifetime, and the worst will attain it only after many lives.

The Bhagavad Gita exhorts Satyameva Jayate (truth alone triumphs) even though there are no mention of Satyameva Jayate anywhere in the Bhagavad Gita.

Chapter 10

What makes the Bhagavad Gita the most important scripture in the world?

Grandson: What makes the Bhagavad Gita the most important scripture in the world?

Grandfather: The Bhagavad Gita is the most important scripture of the Hindus and many millions of others because of the variety of subjects it discusses in its 700 verses.

> The Bhagavad Gita gives each one of us absolute freedom to do whatever we want.
>
> In the Bhagavad Gita, Lord Krishna never judges or orders Arjuna. He only explains to him the pros and cons of every issue, leaving it up to Arjuna whether to follow Krishna's teachings or not.
>
> Lord Krishna did not even influence Arjuna's free will. Arjuna had the right to accept everything Lord Krishna taught or reject everything Lord Krishna taught. In fact, at the end of the Mahabharata, Rishi Veda Vyasa has to teach a very disheartened Arjuna the whole of the Bhagavad Gita again.

The Bhagavad Gita advocates selfless actions (Nishkama Karma). It teaches the importance of annihilating desire and the ego. It teaches different ways to control the mind and the senses.

You can find all of the great teachings of Jesus Christ regarding devotion and oneness with God in the Bhagavad Gita as well. The Bhagavad Gita describes oneness with God in chapters 11–14 and 18 with lines such as "enters into me," "attains me," "abide in me," "realize me," "attains Brahman," among others.

> Not even once does Lord Krishna say: "You will go to hell if you do not follow me or obey what I say," like what we read in other religious scriptures.

The beauty of the Bhagavad Gita is that it requires people to completely change their consciousness, rather than merely changing lifestyles or outward appearances. It advocates a balanced life. Further, it never ever asks anyone to run away from life. Instead, it asks everyone to fully participate in life. Always remember that after the Bhagavad Gita, Arjuna does not become a hermit; instead he fights a very fierce war, annihilating all of his enemies.

Most intellectuals go through the Bhagavad Gita at least once in their lifetime. Aldous Huxley wrote, "The Bhagavad Gita is perhaps the most systematic scripture statement of the perennial philosophy" in his introduction to *The Song of God* by Swami Prabhavananda and Christopher Isherwood. The scripture has won the interest and admiration of such intellectuals as Von Humboldt of Germany and Emerson of America, and has influenced thinkers like Hegel and Schopenhauer. Robert Oppenheimer, the first chairman of the US Atomic Energy Commission, shocked the world when he quoted a couplet from the Gita (11:12) after witnessing the very first atomic explosion test, called Trinity, on July 16, 1945 in New Mexico. Later, in a congressional hearing, Oppenheimer said nuclear bombs reminded him of the Hindu god Vishnu, who said: "I am death, the devourer of all."

Lord Krishna never judges or orders throughout the Bhagavad Gita.

He does not even influence Arjuna's free will.

Arjuna has the right to accept everything Lord Krishna teaches as well as the right to reject everything Lord Krishna teaches.

In fact, at the end of the Mahabharata, Rishi Veda Vyasa has to come and teach a broken hearted Arjuna, the Bhagavad Gita all over again.

Throughout the Bhagavad Gita, you will not see even one verse stating "Unless you obey me you will go to hell."

Chapter 11

Why did Arjuna refuse to fight?

Details	Verse
Arjuna asks Krishna to place his chariot in between two armies.	1:21
Arjuna does not want to fight.	1:28–46
Arjuna drops his bow and arrow and sits in the chariot.	1:47

Grandson: How does the Bhagavad Gita start?

Grandfather: First of all, remember, as I told you before, everything in the Bhagavad Gita is symbolic. I believe the whole Mahabharata epic was written by Rishi Veda Vyasa so that he could educate the whole world about the unwritten laws of the universe.

Are you saying that the Mahabharata War was a symbolic war?

I think so.

> The Mahabharata War was not a bloody war of relatives killing relatives. Instead, it was a symbolic war between right and wrong, good and bad, which is happening within all of us every day.

Rishi Veda Vyasa described this war in such a way as to keep his authorship anonymous. The narration of the Bhagavad Gita is essentially a "question and answer" dialog about every aspect of life between Lord Krishna and the warrior prince Arjuna. Their dialog is seen and heard telepathically by a third person, Sanjaya, the advisor and charioteer of the blind King Dhritarashtra, who then narrates the plot of the book to the king.

First Person	Lord Krishna	God
Second Person	Arjuna	Warrior prince
Third Person	Sanjaya	Advisor of King Dhritarashtra
Fourth Person	Dhritarashtra	Blind king

The first chapter of the Bhagavad Gita starts with the king asking Sanjaya to describe what his sons, the Kauravas, and his brother's sons, the Pandavas, are doing in the battlefield of Kurukshethra. (1:1)

Symbol	What it represents
Kurukshethra	Body and mind
Kauravas	Negative, evil thoughts
Pandavas	Positive, good thoughts
Mahabharata War	War between right and wrong within all of us

After the introduction of the commanders of each army and the blowing of conch shells, Arjuna tells Krishna that he wants to see all of the people assembled to fight. Lord Krishna, as requested, places Arjuna's chariot between the two armies. There, Arjuna sees his grandfather Bhishma, his great Guru Drona, and many of his close relatives and friends, all ready to fight against him.

After seeing all of the people whom he adores and his kinsmen standing to fight, Arjuna is overcome with depression.

Arjuna said:
"O Krishna, just witnessing my own relatives getting ready
to fight and kill each other, my limbs keep shivering, my
body is trembling, my mouth is drying up, and my hair is
standing up.
My bow (Gandiva) is slipping from my hand, and my skin is
burning.
I am unable to keep my composure. I am forgetting myself.
O Krishna, I can see only heartache and misfortune
ahead of me."
(1:28–30)

Arjuna says that he has no desire to fight and that there will
be no point in winning after killing many blood relatives, as well
as his own guru, Drona, and his grandfather, Bhishma. Then,
casting aside his bow and arrow, Arjuna sits down on the seat of
the chariot, his mind overwhelmed with sorrow. (1:47)

Chapter 12

Was the Mahabharata War a symbolic war?

Grandson: Once again, do you think the Mahabharata War was a symbolic war, described so that Rishi Veda Vyasa could cleverly teach us the unwritten laws of the universe?

Grandfather: Oh! My God! You took the words out of my mouth. I believe that the whole story of the Mahabharata and its ferocious war was written by Rishi Veda Vyasa in order to create a proper atmosphere for conveying the unwritten laws of the universe to the world.

To me, the Mahabharata does not describe a ferocious, bloody war of relatives killing relatives for selfish goals, but a war between right and wrong, good and evil, in the minds of everyone on earth. (This is an important subject: you will be amazed to know that the conflict between good and evil is one of the important percepts of the Zoroastrian faith also.)

In my opinion, telling the story through the voices of Lord Krishna and Arjuna was the great sage's means of providing an authoritative look at the ultimate truths he wanted the world to know.

For example, if I were to discuss my thoughts about the US Constitution or the Bill of Rights, not even a fly would listen. But if Supreme Court Chief Justice Roberts were to say something about the US Constitution or the Bill of Rights, all of America will listen. And further: if the President and Chief Justice Roberts discuss the US Constitution with one another, the whole world will want to listen.

The same analogy is applicable regarding the narration of the Bhagavad Gita. If it was written solely from the author's point of view—"Veda Vyasa said so"—it would not have been read by many. But since it was written as a lively conversation between the greatest archer of the world, Prince Arjuna, and the greatest teacher of the world, Lord Krishna, at the outset of the great Mahabharata War, the whole world rejoices in reading it.

Legends say that after Veda Vyasa finished the Mahabharata, Sage Narada compelled him to continue by writing the Srimad Bhagavatam Purana with the help of Lord Ganapati (Ganesha). This would allow even laymen to understand all the teachings of the Bhagavad Gita in a very devotional format.

As I told you before, Rishi Veda Vyasa wrote the epic, the Mahabharata at the request of Sage Narada so that ordinary people could comprehend subtle truths of the universe through a story. Ordinary people are not well versed in intellectual treatises such as the Upanishads and the Darshanas. Without books like the Mahabharata, they would miss out on knowing many of the extremely subtle truths of the universe.

Symbol	What it represents
Chariot	Human body
Lord Krishna	Absolute soul (Paramatman)
Warrior prince Arjuna	Individual soul (Jiva, Jeevatman)
Five horses	The five sense organs, or indriyas
Kauravas	Negative thoughts
Pandavas	Positive thoughts

Taking the Bhagavad Gita symbolically, Lord Krishna is teaching Arjuna how to attain self-realization: first by eradicating his negative thoughts, and then by eradicating all of his thoughts in order to enter a thoughtless state.

Arjuna
(Individual Soul–Atman)
(Jeevatman)

Krishna
(Absolute Soul–God)
(Paramatman)

Chariot
(Human body)

Five horses
(Five sense organs)
(indriyas)

Reins
(Control of senses and
mind)

War
(War with the body
between right and wrong
and good and evil)

Kauravas
(Bad and evil thoughts)

Pandavas
(Good and spiritual
thoughts)

Symbolic chart of the Bhagavad Gita

Bhagavad Gita is a discussion between

First Person (Lord Krishna)

Second Person (warrior Prince Arjuna)

seen and heard
by third person Sanjaya
(advisor and also the charioteer of King
Dhritarashtra)

narrating that to the fourth person
(blind King Dhritarashtra)

Chapter 13

Why is the Bhagavad Gita's point of view so unusual?

Grandson: Why is the Bhagavad Gita's point of view so unusual?

Grandfather: I don't understand your question.

Grandpa, what I meant is this: Veda Vyasa could have just described his ultimate truths directly in poetry or prose. So why did he tell the story in this elaborate way by making Sanjaya telepathically witness Lord Krishna and Arjuna in the battlefield and telling that to the blind king, Dhritarashtra?

Excellent question. All Hindu scriptures are written anonymously in this way. For example, the Ramayana was written from the point of view of a crying bird telling Sage Valmiki the story of Rama and Sita.

I think the ancient Hindu sages did that to avoid ego. I also think they wanted to make sure that the world understood that the things they were writing were the laws of the universe rather than merely their personal opinions. Rishi Veda Vyasa did not want anybody to think that the Bhagavad Gita contained only his personal theories about truth, which is the reason why he might have written the Bhagavad Gita as he did.

Chapter 14

If Hinduism upholds non-violence, why did Lord Krishna ask Arjuna to kill his enemies?

Grandson: You told me earlier that the Bhagavad Gita is a friendly chat between Lord Krishna and his warrior friend Arjuna prior to a major bloody war between two families. You also told me that Lord Krishna advised Arjuna to bear arms and kill his own family. How can you call that a religious book? In Hinduism, don't we also say ahimsa paramo dharma—"non-violence is the ultimate virtue"? It doesn't make any sense at all.

Grandfather: I am happy to hear that very thought-provoking question. To begin with, as I said, I don't believe the Mahabharata War was a family feud. Rather, it was a spiritual war between right and wrong, good and evil, that happens every day in our lives.

I am of the opinion that the whole Mahabharata epic, with its 200,000 verses, was written so that Sage Veda Vyasa could give the world the concise teachings of the 108 Upanishads and 6 Hindu philosophies through a little 700-verse book called the Bhagavad Gita.

As I told you before, Rishi Veda Vyasa wrote the Mahabharata at the request of Sage Narada so that ordinary people could comprehend the subtle truths of the universe through a story. Ordinary people are not well versed in intellectual treatises such as the Upanishads. Without books like the Mahabharata, they would miss out on their wisdom.

But if the Bhagavad Gita contains the truth, does that mean that the words ahimsa paramo dharma don't mean much?

I do not mean to say that at all. Ahimsa paramo dharma is very important in Hinduism. Gandhi used that to emancipate India from the British, winning India's independence without even firing one bullet. So under no condition will I look down on a statement like ahimsa paramo dharma.

At the same time, ahimsa paramo dharma does not appear anywhere in the Bhagavad Gita. Lord Krishna never says that non-violence is the ultimate duty. If he did, there would have been no Mahabharata War.

The verse appears at other places in the Mahabharata. But you only quoted the first part of the verse. The actual verse has two parts:

> "Ahimsa paramo dharma;
> Dharma himsa tathaiva cha."
> Which means:
> Non-violence is the ultimate Dharma.
> So, too, is violence in service of Dharma.

In other words, to preserve dharma (righteousness) and eradicate adharma, a person can resort to violence if non-violent methods fail. Lord Krishna tried his best to avoid a war. But Duryodhana wanted a war so that he could kill all of the Pandavas, and thus war became unavoidable.

Apart from that, Arjuna is a Kshatriya (warrior). As such, it would be impossible for him to run away from his karmic debt and become an ascetic. If he ran away to the Himalayas, he would still have to fight—only instead of fighting a righteous war, he would be fighting for food, women, and shelter. That is the reason why Krishna urges Arjuna to fight.

A girl who is going to be raped by anyone, including by her own husband, has every right to protect herself—even by resorting to extreme violence.

A householder has the rights protect his or her family by whatever means possible.

A country has to defend itself against all foreign aggression. So in day-to-day life, we can never rule out himsa (violence) as a means of protecting dharma. Ahimsa is the best way, but when ahimsa fails, there is nothing wrong with resorting to himsa to protect dharma in all circumstances.

The Mahabharata War was not a
bloody war of relatives
killing relatives;

instead it was a symbolic war
between right and wrong, good
and bad, which is happening within
all of us every day.

Arjuna	Symbolizes	Jeevatman or the immortal soul within the body.
Lord Krishna	Symbolizes	God or Paramatman
Kurukshethra	Symbolizes	Field of action: life
Five horses	Symbolizes	Five sense organs
Pandavas	Symbolizes	Positive spiritual thoughts
Kauravas	Symbolizes	Negative destructive thoughts

Chapter 15

Is Lord Krishna the true God?

Description	Verse
Lord Krishna states that he is the formless God.	9:11
Lord Krishna states that he is the father, mother, ritual, sacrifice, and anything and everything one can think of.	9:16–9:19
Arjuna requests to see Krishna's true form.	11:3–4
Lord Krishna tells Arjuna to see his cosmic form.	11:5
Lord Krishna gives Arjuna special power to see the form.	11:8
Arjuna sees the cosmic form.	11:12–25
All of the Kauravas are dying in the mouth of God.	11:26–27
Krishna asks Arjuna to be an instrument.	11:33–34
Arjuna apologizes to Krishna for treating him as merely a friend, not realizing that he is the almighty God.	11:41–42

Grandson: Grandfather, do you think Lord Krishna is the true God?

Grandfather: I can fully understand why you asked me that question. Even Arjuna was not initially sure about Lord Krishna. He saw Lord Krishna as a friend, as well as a romantic hero of women everywhere. He never thought that Lord Krishna was actually God incarnate.

Lord Krishna was introduced in the Mahabharata as an avatar (incarnation of God) of Lord Vishnu, the second person of the Hindu Trinity. The Bhagavad Gita, however, portrays him as Brahman (God).

Are you a member of the Hare Krishna movement? Is that the reason why you are saying Lord Krishna is the true God?

I am not a member of ISKON (the Hare Krishna movement). I am only stating facts about the Bhagavad Gita. All of Arjuna's doubts about the true nature of Lord Krishna vanish the moment Lord Krishna shows him his "cosmic form" or "formless form" (Viswaroopa).

> Lord Krishna said:
> "Arjuna, you cannot see me with your eyes, therefore I am giving you divine sight. Behold my supreme Yoga power."
> (11:8)

Then Arjuna saw the entire universe with its many divisions resting together in the body of the God of gods. In verses 11:14–31, Arjuna describes that "cosmic form of God" in detail. Arjuna even apologizes to Lord Krishna for doubting his true nature.

> Arjuna said:
> "Please forgive me for treating you as a friend and addressing you as 'Krishna', 'Yadava', 'friend'. Out of total ignorance I have treated you as an ordinary friend. O The great infinite, infallible Lord, please forgive me."
> (11:41–42)

Thus we have to conclude that the Almighty came down as Lord Krishna. In his own words, he will come down again and again in different forms whenever the world needs him.

All through the Bhagavad Gita, Lord Krishna says "I am the

Way" and "Come to me". He is a teacher, leader, hero, protector, philosopher, teacher, lover, and friend all rolled into one.

> Lord Krishna said:
> "Fools ridicule me since I took the human form, not understanding my mystical nature as the Lord of all beings, the Brahman itself."
> (9:11)

> Lord Krishna said:
> "Arjuna, please know that I am the ritual, I am the sacrifice, and the offering. I am the medicine, the mantra, the offering to the ancestors. I am the butter and the fire and the offering.
> I am the father of this universe, its mother, and the grandfather. I am knowledge (jnana) and the syllable Aum. I am also the Rig, the Sama, and the Yajur Vedas.
> I am the supreme goal of everyone, the Lord, witness, abode, refuge, friend. I am the creation and the annihilation.
> I am the basis of everything, the resting place. I am the origin. I radiate heat, and I withhold and send forth the rain. I am immortality, and I am also death. I am that which you see and that which you do not see. I am that which exists and that which does not exist."
> (9:16–19)

Hindus respect all religions.

Hindu scriptures do not profess a monopoly on God, Truth, or salvation.

All those things are universal and as such no religion can proclaim a monopoly on those things.

That is the reason why rishis wrote:

"Let Noble Thoughts come to us from all sides."—Rig Veda 1-89

Chapter 16

Summary of the eighteen
chapters of the Bhagavad Gita

Grandson: May I have a short summary of every chapter of the Bhagavad Gita? I don't want to know any lengthy details—I have to study for my classes, so I'm short of time.

Grandfather: I fully understand. As I said at the outset, my idea is not to bombard you with every minute detail about the Bhagavad Gita. I wanted to just give you an idea of what Lord Krishna says about each subject. If you want to have a word for word translation of the Bhagavad Gita, there are thousands available in the market.

	Yoga	Verses	Summary
1	Arjuna Vishada Yoga	46	Arjuna asks Lord Krishna to move his chariot between the two armies. Seeing that he must kill many of his relatives to win the war, he becomes depressed and refuses to fight.
2	Sankhya Yoga	72	Lord Krishna educates Arjuna about the immortality of the soul and tells him that he will never inherit sin (paap) by doing his duty. Lord Krishna also says: "So far I have spoken to you about the wisdom of Sankhya philosophy," and discusses the idea of an enlightened person.

3	Karma Yoga	43	Lord Krishna explains everything about karma (actions), including the importance of selfless actions (Nishkama Karma) and how these are the best ways for a human to achieve salvation.
4	Jnana Karma Sanyasa Yoga	42	Lord Krishna reveals that he is an avatar of God, and that whenever there is a decline in dharma and a rise in adharma, he is born to protect the good, destroy the wicked, and establish righteousness.
5	Karma Sanyasa Yoga	29	A very confused Arjuna asks Lord Krishna whether it is better to forgo action or to act. Lord Krishna answers that acting and not acting have the same goal, but that acting in Karma Yoga is superior.
6	Dhyana Yoga	47	Lord Krishna explains the different techniques by which one can control the mind.
7	Jnana Vijnana Yoga	30	Lord Krishna describes nature in vivid detail.
8	Akshara Brahma Yoga	28	Lord Krishna discusses death and the techniques of pranayama. He also describes the differences between the material and spiritual worlds.
9	Raja–Vidya–Raja–Guhya Yoga	34	Lord Krishna introduces Raja Yoga as a royal secret. He also describes how he creates, maintains, and annihilates the entire universe again and again through his maya (power of illusions).

10	Vibhuti Yoga	42	Lord Krishna declares himself to be the Brahman, the God which is the cause of all material and spiritual existence, by saying: "Among Vedas, I am Sama Veda, among indriyas; I am the mind." Lord Krishna informs Arjuna that there is nothing but God, and that everything else is maya (illusion).
11	Viswaroopa–Darshana Yoga	55	Arjuna asks, "Who are you, Krishna? I want to see your true form." Lord Krishna shows Arjuna his Viswaroopa (cosmic formless form), which emits the radiance of a thousand suns and contains all other beings and material in existence.
12	Bhakti Yoga	20	Arjuna asks an excellent question: should people worship God as Nirguna Brahman (a formless, nameless God) or as Saguna Brahman (a God with attributes, such as Lord Krishna)? Lord Krishna says that both will attain the same goal, but that praying and surrendering to him is the much easier path.
13	Kshetra–Kshetrajna Vibhaga Yoga	35	Lord Krishna discusses the differences between the perishable material body and the immortal soul (Atman). Many verses in this chapter discuss Brahman—God.

14	Gunatraya Vibhaga Yoga	27	Lord Krishna explains in detail about the three gunas (modes of mind) and also tells Arjuna that first he has to develop sattva guna, but that in the end, he should go above the gunas. Only a person who transcends all three gunas can attain salvation.
15	Purushottama Yoga	20	Lord Krishna describes the upside down tree of Samsara (repeated cycles of birth, death, and reincarnation) with its roots above and branches below. According to him, this tree should be chopped with the "axe of detachment" to attain salvation.
16	Dhaivasura– Sampat– Vibhaga Yoga	24	Lord Krishna discusses the people who state that this world is unreal and created through lust, with no foundation or any God in control. According to Lord Krishna, these people are governed by Kama (lust), Krodha (anger), and Ahamkara (ego).
17	Shradd- hatraya- Vibhaga Yoga	28	Lord Krishna categorizes faith, thoughts, deeds, food, meditation, and charity according to the three gunas.

| 18 | Sanyasa Yoga | 78 | Lord Krishna categorizes jnana, karma, intellect, courage, happiness, and caste according to the three gunas. In verse 66, Lord Krishna asks Arjuna to abandon all duties (dharma) and surrender to him, and he will deliver Arjuna from all bonds of karma. At the very end of this chapter, Sanjaya says to King Dhritarashtra: "Wherever there is Lord Krishna, the master of all yogas, and the archer Arjuna, there alone will be fortune, victory, well-being, and righteousness. This my opinion." (18:78) |

Chapter 17

Is the Bhagavad Gita based on Sankhya philosophy?

Details	Verse
Talks about Sankhya philosophy in this verse	2:39
People who follow Sankhya philosophy and people who follow Karma Yoga have the same result	3:3
Sankhya philosophy and Yoga are one	5:4–5
Eight basic elements, according to Sankhya	7:4
Arjuna wants to know about Purusha and Prakriti	13:1
Purusha and Prakriti (Sankhya philosophy)	13:20–23
Lord Krishna says: "Among Siddhas (perfected beings), I am Sage Kapila (the founder of Sankhya philosophy)"	10:26

The gunas, associated with Sankhya, are further discussed in following chapters:

Subject	Verses
Upside-down tree	15:2–4
Tapas	17:17–19
Worship	17:1–5,
Food	17:8–10
Gifts	17:20–22
Sacrifice	17:11–13 and 18:9
Jnana	18:20–22

Karma	18:23–29
Intellect	18:30–32
Courage	18:33–35
Happiness	18:37–39

Grandson: Grandfather, do you think the Bhagavad Gita is based on Sankhya philosophy?

Grandfather: I am not 100 percent certain that the Bhagavad Gita is based on Sankhya philosophy. Still, I see so many verses in the Bhagavad Gita mention either Sankhya or things associated with Sankhya such as Purusha and Prakriti, as well as the three gunas (tendencies of the mind).

As I said earlier, Hindus have six philosophies called the Darshanas, including Sankhya philosophy. I have never seen any mention of the other five Hindu philosophies in the Bhagavad Gita, except for Vedanta, which is mentioned in two verses.

What is Sankhya philosophy?

Sankhya is based upon the Sanskrit word sankhya, which means number, or in a literal sense, "discrimination between truth and untruth". The term sankhya also means perfect knowledge.

Sankhya does not accept the idea of an Absolute Principle or God behind creation. According to Sankhya, life on earth is not a miracle worked by God but a creative process that passes through different phases of change and transformation.

According to Sankhya, there are only two things in this world: Purusha (energy) and Prakriti (matter). Lord Krishna says that Prakriti manifests as Purusha, and in the end Prakriti merges back into Purusha. He also discusses the three gunas (sattva, rajas, and tamas) and the eight basic elements out of which the whole universe is made: earth, water, fire, air, ether, mind, intellect, and egoism. (7:4).

> Lord Krishna said:
> "Arjuna, I have spoken to you about the wisdom of Sankhya philosophy. Now please hear about the wisdom of Karma Yoga, the path of selfless actions (Nishkama Karma), the path of freedom from all bondage."
> (2:39)

> Lord Krishna said:
> "Arjuna, there are two classes of men in the world who attain self-realization. First, there are the people who follow Sankhya philosophy and try to realize truth through empirical, philosophical speculation, and there are the others who try to realize truth by following Karma Yoga, the path of selfless actions."
> (3:3)

> Lord Krishna said:
> "Those who are ignorant will say that Sankhya philosophy and Karma Yoga, the path of selfless actions, are totally different. Knowledgeable people never say that. Anyone who practices either of these will get the same result. Whatever you achieve by following Sankhya philosophy, you can also achieve through Karma Yoga, the path of selfless actions. One who understands this sees things as they are."
> (5:4–5)

Sankhya philosophy and Karma Yoga are one and the same, as far as the final result is concerned. That is the reason why I feel that Sankhya philosophy is the basic philosophy of the Bhagavad Gita.

Apart from that, Lord Krishna specially uses the Sanskrit word sankhya in many verses. He could very well use the word jnana to mean the same thing, but he does not. He also describes many aspects of Purusha, Prakriti, and the gunas elsewhere, referring to the gunas in more than thirty verses. Chapter 14 of the Bhagavad Gita is even called Gunatraya Vibhaga Yoga, which means the "Yoga of the division of the three gunas". In this chapter, Lord Krishna analyzes the gunas in very minute detail.

Lord Krishna said:
"Being misled by the three gunas, the whole world does not recognize me, who am above all three gunas and am imperishable. This divine energy of mine consisting of three gunas is difficult to overcome. Only those who surrender to me and take refuge in me can surpass these three gunas."
(7:13–14)

Lord Krishna said:
"Arjuna, please understand that Purusha and Prakriti have no beginning and that the gunas arise from Prakriti. Prakriti is the cause of all the material in the world. Purusha is the cause of our experience of happiness and distress. Purusha situated in Prakriti experiences the three gunas. That person who fully understands Purusha, Prakriti, and the three gunas will not be born again, regardless of his present position."
(13:19–23)

Lord Krishna said:
"Fools cannot understand how the immortal soul (Atman) can quit his body, nor understand how Atman enjoys life under the influence of the three gunas. Only the wise can know this through the eyes of knowledge."
(15:10)

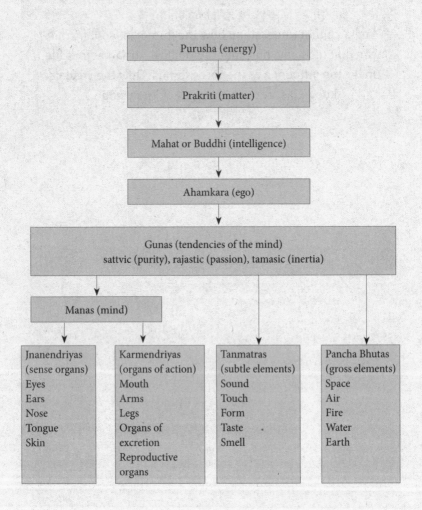

Sankhya philosophy and everything associated with it such as Purusha (energy), Prakriti (matter), and the gunas (innate qualities and tendencies) are mentioned in many verses in the Bhagavad Gita.

There is no mention of the other **five philosophies** anywhere in the Bhagavad Gita except Vedanta in two verses (15.5 and 18.13).

There is no mention of the **Atharva Veda** in the Bhagavad Gita.

It only mentions the first three Vedas:

Rig Veda, Yajur Veda, and **Sama Veda** in many verses.

The word **Upanishad** is not mentioned by name in any of the 700 verses of the Bhagavad Gita.

There is no such thing as **Samkhya** or **Sankhya Yoga**.
We only have **Sankhya philosophy**.

Lord Krishna merely used the word **sankhya** throughout the Bhagavad Gita.

Sankhya is one of the six Darshanas or philosophical systems. It was founded by Rishi Kapila. This philosophy is somewhat atheistic in nature since no god is mentioned anywhere within it. The Bhagavad Gita starts with this philosophy (2.39).

Lord Krishna said: "People who follow Sankhya philosophy and people who follow Karma Yoga will have the same result" (3.3). Lord Krishna only said sankhya. He never said Sankhya Yoga.

All human beings are born with three gunas (innate qualities and tendencies).

Sattva	Balance, joy, harmony, intelligence
Rajas	Greed, passion, change, movement
Tamas	Inactivity, recklessness, delusion

Lord Krishna advises us to develop the **sattva guna first** and then later **to transcend all gunas**. At that stage a person will enter the stage of an **enlightened person** who will be above all dualities such hot and cold and pleasure and pain.

The Bhagavad Gita is based on Sankhya philosophy since many verses in the Bhagavad Gita mention Purusha, Prakriti, and gunas associated with Sankhya Yoga.

Six Hindu philosophies are:

1	Mimamsa	Beginning of Vedas. Deals with "reflection" or "critical investigation".
2	Sankhya	An atheistic philosophy dealing with Purusha (energy), Prakriti, (matter), and gunas.
3	Yoga	Emphasizes on meditation, contemplation, and self-realization.
4	Nyaya	Based on logic. Nyaya means "rules", "method", or "judgment".
5	Vaisheshika	Based on metaphysics, epistemology, logic, and ethics.
6	Vedanta	End of Vedas. Divided into Advaita (only one) and Dwaita (two).

Chapter 18

What is Karma Yoga?

Details	Verse
Details about karma	3:4–9
Selfless actions (Nishkama Karma)	3:18–20, 25
Nothing to do or gain in three worlds	3:22–24
Karma does not affect God	3:14
More discussion of karma	4:16–23
Parodharma (someone else's duty)	3:35
Submitting karma to God	5:10
God does not create karma for anyone	5:14
God does not accept anyone's punya or paap (sin)	5:15
He who thinks he is not acting	18:17

Grandson: What is karma?

Grandfather: Karma originated from the root word *kar*, meaning "to do, make, perform, accomplish, cause, or effect". In a nutshell, karma means both actions and the result of a person's actions.

Even thinking is considered to be karma. We do karma all the time. When we breathe, it is karma. When we think, it is karma. The karma we do dictates our past, present, and future. It is impossible to live without taking any action.

What is the law of karma?

Karma is about all that a person has done, is doing, and will do in the future. Karma is not considered to be a punishment or a reward. To some extent, it is almost like Newton's third law of motion: "For every action, there is an equal and opposite reaction."

Karma also means the cycle of cause and effect. According to the theory of karma, what happens to a person happens because he or she caused it with his or her actions in this life or in previous lives.

Karma is an important part of Hinduism, Jainism, Buddhism, and Sikhism. According to the theory of karma, good actions as well as good thoughts bring forth good karmic results, and bad actions and well as bad thoughts bring forth bad karmic results. Thus one's thoughts and actions dictate one's happiness and unhappiness.

What is Samsara?

Samsara means the repeated cycles of birth, life, death, and reincarnation caused by the consequences of one's actions in the past, present, and future. Hinduism, Jainism, Buddhism, Sikhism, and even Taoism believe in Samsara.

What is Karma Yoga?

Karma Yoga means attaining salvation through the path of selfless actions (Nishkama Karma).

Can you describe yoga in detail? I'm still not sure what yoga means or what the concept of Hindu salvation is.

The word yoga came the root word *yuj*, meaning "to unite or bond." So yoga means union with God, or salvation.

Sage Pathanjali wrote in the Patanjali Yoga Sutra: "Yoga Chitta Vrithi Nirodha."

Yoga	Union with the divine
Chitta Vrithi	Mental vibrations
Nirodha	Stoppage

Thus "Yoga Chitta Vrithi Nirodha" means to unite with the divine means to stop all mental activity.

Salvation in Hinduism could also be called self-realization: to realize that one is indeed the Atman within the body, and to relinquish the false belief that one is the perishable material body. That is the reason why Hindu salvation is also known as moksha, meaning emancipation, liberation, or release from the cycles of birth, death, and rebirth.

Salvation in Hindusim can be achieved through one of the four paths we have discussed: Jnana, Karma, Raja, or Bhakti Yoga.

What did Lord Krishna say about action or Karma Yoga?

The Gita allots three chapters and 113 verses to explain Karma Yoga. Some of the important points are:

1) No man will reach a state of Nishkarmata (freedom from actions) by shunning or abstaining from actions.
2) Action is the nature of all beings in creation.
3) He who controls his desires of the flesh and does selfless actions is an honourable man.
4) To do actions without seeking profit will ensure salvation for you.
5) As God, there is nothing Krishna must do in the three worlds, and there is nothing in the three worlds he needs or can't get. Still, he works all the time.
6) A man should do his duty (svadharma). A man will meet with disaster if he does someone else's duty. Svadharma, however despicable it may be, is better than someone else's duty.
7) He who performs unattached actions by surrendering them to me will not be touched by sin, just as water drops on a lotus leaf do not wet it.
8) Actions do not taint Krishna, nor does he have any desire for the fruits of actions. No action is binding on someone who understands Krishna in this way.

Lord Krishna said:
"God is not responsible for anyone's sinful (paap) activities or pious (punya) activities. People are mistaken about this since their knowledge is covered by ignorance."
(5:15)

God is not responsible for someone's wrong activities or right activities.
God does not influence the free will of any man.

God does not even try to influence Arjuna's free will. He has the freedom to reject everything Lord Krishna teaches as well as to accept everything Lord Krishna teaches.

Lord Krishna said:
"God does not decide the karma each one of us should do, nor does he induce people to act, nor does he create fruits of any action. Each person acts according to his vasanas (past and present perceptions of mind)."
(5:14)

God is not the creator of karma. Karma is created by each individual's personal thoughts and actions.

Chapter 19

What is Nishkama Karma, and why is that the best path?

Details	Verse
You only have the right to act	2:47
Selfless actions (Nishkama Karma)	2:49–51, 3:18–20

Grandson: What is the basis of Karma Yoga?

Grandfather: Selfless action, or Nishkama Karma, is the basis of Karma Yoga. One of the best methods to attain salvation or self-realization is to do selfless actions.

When we do selfless actions, we should not even look forward to a "thank you" card. That way, we can eradicate ego, as well as any attachment to the results of our actions. Lord Krishna repeatedly stresses the idea of working without any attachment. All actions should be done as a service or duty, and we have to perform them while remaining detached from all possible outcomes.

> Lord Krishna said:
> "You only have the right to act. At the same time, you do not have the right to the fruits of actions. You should not act out of motivation for the fruits of actions, and you should never be inactive at any time."
> (2:47)

Lord Krishna is telling us not to brag about the things we do for anyone. We should take it as our privilege to serve whenever we help anyone in any manner.

> In the Holy Bible, Jesus Christ says: "But when you give to the poor, do not let your left hand know what your right hand is doing." (Matthew 6:3)

Both Lord Krishna as well as Jesus Christ are telling us that we should do things without looking for any compliments or rewards. The moment we look forward to any reward, good as well as bad, our action becomes tainted.

In Karma Yoga, when we perform selfless actions, no effort is ever lost and there is no adverse effect. Even the slightest practice of this discipline protects one from all great dangers.

> Lord Krishna said:
> "Arjuna, being fixed in Yoga, perform your duty (svadharma), abandoning all attachments to success or failure. Such equanimity of the mind in success as well as in failure is what is called Karma Yoga.
> Arjuna, any action or service done with a selfish motive to enjoy the results is far inferior to selfless service (Nishkarmata). Those who act because they are motivated by desire for the fruits of actions are in truth very unhappy. A person who knows how to act this way gets rid of both good and bad karmic debt. Acting without becoming attached to the fruits of actions is called Karma Yoga.
> Therefore, devote yourself to Karma Yoga.
> Those who have become established in Karma Yoga, those who have renounced the fruits of the actions, are released from the bondage of Samsara and attain the blissful divine state."
> (2:48–51)

Arjuna asks a very thought-provoking question:
"O Krishna, if you say knowledge (jnana) is superior to
action (karma), then why are you forcing me to commit this
terrible deed of waging a war against my family?
Krishna, you confuse my intelligence with conflicting
messages. Therefore, instead of telling me many things,
please tell me just the one thing that will be most beneficial
to me."
Lord Krishna replied:
"O Arjuna, as I have explained to you previously, there
are two ways to lead a fulfilling life. One is the path of
knowledge (jnana), and the other is the path of selfless
action (Nishkama Karma)."
(3:1-3)

The path of knowledge (Jnana Yoga) is best suited for the deep
thinkers who like to contemplate and reason. The path of selfless
action is best suited for those who are active and like to work hard.

Lord Krishna said:
"By abstaining from action, nobody can achieve freedom
from action, nor can one attain perfection by abandonment
or renunciation of all actions.
No one can refrain from doing something, not even for a
second. Everyone is forced to act all the time due to the
influence of the three gunas.
A person who has stopped working and whose mind dwells
on sense objects deludes himself and is called a hypocrite.
However, one who tries to control the senses by the mind
and without attachment to sensual pleasures engages in
selfless actions (Nishkama Karma), which are superior to
others."
(3:4-7)

A person excels in life when he disciplines the senses with the mind and engages in work without getting attached to results of actions.

Lord Krishna said:
"Arjuna, please perform your prescribed duty (svadharma), for doing so is better than inaction. One cannot even maintain one's body or mind without any action. All actions done in this world are binding (that is a karmic debt) unless done as a sacrifice to God. Perform your prescribed duties as a sacrifice to God, and this way you will not be attached to the results of your actions, and you will remain free from any bondage."
(3:8–9)

Lord Krishna said:

"Those who conduct their duties according to my commands, with full faith, without envy and egoless, are also released from all bondage of actions."

However, those who out of envy disregard my teachings and do not practice them are deluded and deprived of knowledge. Such people have indeed lost understanding and their goal in life.

Even a wise man acts according to the nature he is born with as well as that which he has acquired in this world. Everyone follows his or her acquired nature. What will repression of the senses accomplish?

Likes and dislikes in relation to the sense objects are deeply rooted in the senses and as such, unavoidable. One should not be controlled by them, since they are obstacles in the path of self-realization.

It is always better to perform one's prescribed duties (svadharma), even though faulty, rather than engage in another person's duty (parodharma)."

Arjuna asked:

"Krishna, by what influence does one act improperly, even unwillingly, as if forced to do things against one's own convictions?"

Lord Krishna replied:

"Arjuna, this force that makes people act is lust, is born out of *rajas*. Later, this force transforms into anger. Know that this anger is sinful and injurious to the person.

As the fire is covered by smoke, as a mirror is covered by dust, and an embryo by the womb, so one's proper understanding of truth (jnana) is covered by lust (kama).

O Arjuna, even a wise man's vision is obscured by the perpetual enemy in the form of lust, which is never satisfied, and which burns like fire.

This lust is seated in the senses, mind, and intelligence. From there it influences the immortal soul, confusing it and covering its capability to understand.

O Arjuna, therefore at the very outset one should control his senses (indriyas) and give up on his lust that destroys knowledge.

The wise say that the senses are superior to sense objects and that the mind is superior to the senses. Intellect is superior to the mind and superior to the intellect is the immortal soul within the body.

Arjuna, knowing that the immortal soul is superior to intellect, please control the mind with intellect. In this way, you can destroy the unconquerable, vicious enemy in the form of lust."

(3:31-43)

Akarma means "inaction". There are those who, under the distorted pretext of becoming a sanyasi or yogi, become lazy and give up work altogether. Their akarma (inaction) falls under the category of "tamasic" inactivity—in other words, delusory and selfish action.

Lord Krishna said:
"One who does selfless actions,
one who performs his duty without
attachment, surrendering all his
actions to God, is not stained or
infected by evil, as the lotus leaf is
untouched by water."
(5:10)

In the Holy Bible, (Matthew 6:3) Jesus said:
"But when you give to the poor, do not let your left
hand know what your right hand is doing."

One of the best ways to eradicate karmic
debt and achieve salvation is to do selfless
actions (Nishkama Karma).

Lord Krishna said:
"Arjuna, I have nothing to do
in all three worlds, nor there is
anything to gain in all three worlds.
Despite that, I constantly
act all the time."
(3:22)

The worst thing anyone can do is to sit idle.
The mind is a very powerful thing.
The idle mind is indeed a devil's paradise.

Lord Krishna taught us that action is better than inaction.

A person cannot attain spiritual maturity by renouncing actions because even breathing is an action.

So we are forced to work continuously in a selfless manner (Nishkama Karma) until we attain self-realization.

Chapter 20

Are material things important?

Details	Verse
Everything will come and go.	2:14

Grandson: Are material things important?

Grandfather: Everything will come and go in our lives. Just as we cannot control waves in the sea, we cannot control the ups and downs in our lives.

At the very outset of the Mahabharata War, Lord Krishna said the following to Arjuna:

> Lord Krishna said:
> "Arjuna, everything comes and goes in life. Happiness and unhappiness are temporary experiences that rise from sense perception. Heat and cold, pleasure and pain, will come and go. They never last forever. So do not get attached to them."
> (2:14)

Good and bad things will come and go in our lives. We have no control over them. Things never work out as we expect. That is the reason why we have to give up expectations and go with the flow of life. Throughout the Bhagavad Gita, Lord Krishna brought up the pointlessness of giving undue importance to material things. The more we remain attached to material things as well as people, the more we will suffer.

Only the things that originate within us have lasting value. We should be contented as we are. We should be happy as God made us. Comparing our lives with everyone else's lives will only bring forth misery. Jealousy and depression will take over when we believe the myth that the grass is always greener on the other side of the fence.

When we are taken over by envy, we believe that other people have the very best while we have very little. The fact of the matter is that we have no idea what others are going through in their lives.

Before you say to God, "I want to be just like him or her;" please ask yourself what you are asking of God.

Sometimes the pretty girl whom you become jealous of, whom the world adores, may be suffering from diseases, or may have a drug or alcohol addiction, or may be a victim of abuse. So God will laugh at you if you tell God that you want to be just like her.

In brief, we are forced to become spiritual for our own sake in order to have a peaceful life. Of course, Rome was not built in a day, and it takes years to mature spiritually. Initially, we have to take baby steps. But one day, that will happen in our lives. It is a gluttonous worm that one day becomes a beautiful butterfly. Similarly, it is a very materialistic person who will one day become a yogi.

What Lord Krishna said to Arjuna at the outset of the Mahabharata War—*everything will come and go in our lives, so do not get attached to them*—is still applicable today.

Everything in life comes and goes.
We have no control over it.

Lord Krishna said:
"Arjuna, everything comes and goes
in life. Happiness and unhappiness
are temporary experiences that rise
from sense perception. Heat and
cold, pleasure and pain, will come
and go. They never last forever. So
do not get attached to them."
(2:14)

Good and bad things will come and go in our lives.
We have no control over them. Things never
work out the way we expect. That is the reason why
we have to give up expectations and
go with the flow of life.

King Janaka told
Sage Suka:

"You can possess things,
as long as you are not
possessed by them."

Meaning that there is nothing wrong
with amassing wealth or materials,
as long as you are not overjoyed when
you receive them or sad when you lose
them, and as long as you use them
for unselfish motives like using them
to give charity to the poor and sick.

Chapter 21

Is the creation and annihilation of the universe really cyclical and never-ending?

Details	Verse
Lord Krishna discusses the creation and destruction of the universe.	9:17
Brahma's day	8:17
Brahma's night	8:18
Annihilation of the universe	8:19
Rebirth of the universe	8:20
Creation came out of food. Food came out of rain. From yatnya (sacrifice) came rain. Yatnya came out of karmas.	3:13–16
The eight basic elements	7:4
All creation came from me	10:8
I am the cause of all creation	10:39
Process of creation	14:3–4

Grandson: Many Christians believe the earth is only 6,000 years old. What do Hindus believe?

Grandfather: Excellent question. It is true that many Christians believe God created the world in six literal days roughly 4,000 years before the birth of Jesus Christ, and that he destroyed the world with a global flood during the time of Noah.

However, when other religions talk in terms of thousands of years of history, Hinduism alone thinks in terms of trillions of years.

Carl Sagan, the great American astronomer, was intrigued by "Hindu creation and destruction concepts," since they deal with the idea of the repeated cyclical creation and annihilation of the universe, as well as a trillion-year time scale.

Dr Carl Sagan, in his very popular book *Cosmos*, wrote that Hinduism is the only religion in the world dedicated to the idea that the cosmos itself undergoes an immense, indeed an infinite, number of deaths and rebirths.

When the Shoemaker-Levy 9 comet hit Jupiter on July 16, 1994, everyone rejoiced and astronomers cheered all over the world. I am sure that during that jubilation, nobody thought about whether a comet many times bigger than Shoemaker-Levy 9 might be poised to hit the earth some time in the future!

If a comet or meteor hits the earth one day, we will know about it only months before. After all, it was amateur astronomers Shoemaker and Levy who found out about their comet only six months before it hit Jupiter.

If a comet the size of Shoemaker-Levy 9 hit the earth, it would mean that several millions of pounds of rock up to 2.5 square miles in size would strike earth at a speed of 134,000 miles per hour, producing a surface impact temperature of 53,550 degrees Fahrenheit. (The sun's surface temperature is only 10,350 degrees Fahrenheit.) Instantly, the temperature of the earth would rise by an average of 30 to 40 degrees, melting the ice at the poles and flooding the world. Additionally, the earth would be covered by 100- or 200- mile-high levels of dust. That dust cover would turn the world into a piece of ice, killing all of the plants and animals.

Some scientists associated with NASA believe that an asteroid-like object called 2000 SG344, discovered on September 29, 2000, has a one in 417 chance of colliding with the earth between 2069 and 2113. This may never happen, but just speculating about it should make us realize that nothing is permanent in life.

According to the Big Bang Theory, the universe came into existence about 15 billion years ago after an explosion of hydrogen gas. Hindu scriptures state that the creation and destruction of the universe is a continuous, cyclical process that takes place over trillions of years. It never had a beginning and it will never have an end. This earth we see has been created and destroyed many times, and the cyclical process of creation and destruction is eternal.

In Hindu scriptures, this perpetual creation and destruction of the universe is known as leela. Leela is a Sanskrit word, meaning "the child-like expression of God".

The Bhagavad Gita discusses the creation and annihilation of the universe in many verses.

> Lord Krishna said:
> "In the beginning of time, or Kalpa, I create everything, and at the end of time, or Kalpa, the whole creation merges in me. By my will the whole universe is created and annihilated again and again."
> (9:7)

Now I am confused. You have to explain to me what Kalpa means.

I know what you mean. Time in Hinduism is measured in Yugas. According to Hindu cosmology, the whole universe is created and destroyed within a time period of four Yugas that lasts for 4,320,000 years.

As the earth goes through the seasons—summer, spring, winter, and autumn—each Yuga involves gradual changes to the earth and to the consciousness of mankind, passing from the

Golden Age to a complete Dark Age.

The four Yugas are as follows:

Yuga	Duration	Relative size
Krita or Satya Yuga	1,728,000 years	(4 x Kali Yuga)
Treta Yuga	1,296,000 years	(3 x Kali Yuga)
Dvapara Yuga	864,000 years	(2 x Kali Yuga)
Kali Yuga	432,000 years	

1 Maha Yuga	4 Yugas	4,320,000 years
1 Kalpa	1000 Maha Yugas	4,320,000,000 years
1 day of Brahma	1 Kalpa	4,320,000,000 years
1 night of Brahma	1 Kalpa	4,320,000,000 years
1 whole day of Brahma	2 Kalpas	8,640,000,000 years

The life of Brahma, the God of Creation, will last for 311.04 trillion human years. After that, another Brahma will come. Even Lord Brahma will not live forever.

When did the Kali Yuga start?

In general, we believe that the Kali Yuga started thirty-five years after the conclusion of the Mahabharata War, after Parikshit, the grandson of Arjuna, ascended the throne in Hastinapura and became the king.

But the actual date of the beginning of the Kali Yuga remains shrouded in mystery. We have no way of knowing the exact date. According to the astronomer and mathematician Aryabhatta, the Kali Yuga started in 3102 BC. He finished his book *Aryabhattiya* in 499 CE, in which he gave the exact year of the beginning of Kali Yuga as 3102 BC.

Thus after 427, 000 years, the Kali Yuga will come to an end and the Satya Yuga will start all over again. Lord Krishna dealt with the creation and annihilation of the universe in many verses.

> Lord Krishna said:
> "A day of Lord Brahma, the God of Creation, lasts for a thousand Yugas (4.3 billion years) or one Kalpa, and his night lasts for another thousand Yugas (4.3 billion years) or one Kalpa.
> Arjuna, at the beginning of Brahma's day, all living beings manifest from the unmanifest state. When the night falls, they merge into the unmanifest again.
> Over and over, when Brahma's day arrives, all living entities come into being, and with the arrival of Brahma's night, all of them are annihilated.
> Yet higher than this unmanifest nature, which is eternal, is the supreme nature which is never annihilated. When all in this world is annihilated, that part remains as it is."
> (8:17–20)

By stating that even Lord Brahma will die one day, Hinduism tells the world that only God is eternal, while everything else will come and go. In other words, everything in life is temporary. So if things are going well, enjoy it, because it won't last forever. And if things are going badly, don't worry. That can't last forever either.

When other religions talk about thousands of years, Hinduism alone talks about trillions of years.

We are in the Kali Yuga now. As the earth goes through seasons such as summer, spring, winter, and the autumn, each Yuga involves gradual changes in which the earth and the consciousness of mankind as a whole passes from a Golden Age to a complete Dark Age.

Four Yugas are as follows:		
Krita or Satya Yuga	1,728,000 years	Four times Kali Yuga
Treta Yuga	1,296,000 years	Three times Kali Yuga
Dvapara Yuga	864,000 years	Twice Kali Yuga
Kali Yuga	432,000 years	

One Maha Yuga	Four Yugas	4,320,000 years
One Kalpa	1000 Maha Yugas	4,320,000 years
Lifespan of Lord Brahma	311,04 trillion years	

Lord Krishna said:

"In the beginning of Kalpa (4,320,000,000 years), I create everything, and at the end of Kalpa, the whole creation merges in me. By my will the whole universe is created and annihilated again and again."

(9:7)

Dr Carl Sagan in his very popular book *Cosmos* wrote that Hinduism is the only religion in the world dedicated to the idea that the cosmos itself undergoes an immense, indeed an infinite number of deaths and rebirths.

Chapter 22

What is an avatar?

Details	Verse
Details about the avatar (incarnation of God)	4: 4–9

Grandson: What is an avatar?

Grandfather: Avatar is a Sanskrit word literally meaning "descent"—the descent of God to the earth. An avatar can come in any form and does not necessarily always have to be a human being. The concept of an avatar is found in both Hinduism and Sikhism. Hindus even consider Lord Buddha an avatar.

Is Lord Krishna an avatar?

Lord Krishna is indeed considered an avatar of God. Lord Krishna is recognized as the eighth incarnation of Lord Vishnu. Additionally, by showing the Viswaroopa (cosmic formless form) to Arjuna in the eleventh chapter of the Bhagavad Gita, Lord Krishna proves that he is indeed the personification of God, the Brahman.

What is the purpose of an avatar?

Lord Krishna answered that question very clearly in the Bhagavad Gita.

> Lord Krishna said:
> "Whenever there is a decline in dharma (righteousness)
> and an outbreak of adharma (non-righteousness), I
> descend to protect the good, to annihilate the wicked, and
> to establish righteousness. I am born from age to age."
> (4:7–8)

How many avatars are there?

Lord Vishnu has ten major avatars, known as the Dasa Avatars, as well as twelve minor avatars. Some Puranas describe Balarama, Lord Krishna's brother in the Mahabharata, as the ninth avatar. After Buddhism became popular, the Sanskrit poet Jaya Deva replaced Balarama with Buddha as the ninth avatar in his famous poem *Gita Govinda* around 1200 CE. Dr Radhakrishnan also did the same in his books.

Among the three major Hindu gods (Lord Brahma, Lord Vishnu, and Lord Shiva), only Lord Vishnu takes avatars.

What are the Dasa Avatars?

The Dasa Avatars, in order, are:

No.	Name	Form	Description
1	Matsya	Fish	God incarnated as a fish to rescue Sage Manu (the Hindu equivalent of Noah) from the floods. Matsya is associated with the beginning of the world.
2	Kurma	Tortoise	God incarnated as a turtle to raise the mountain which devas (angels) and asuras (demons) were mining for the nectar of immortality. The mountain was sinking, so Lord Vishnu became a turtle and rested the mountain on his back.

3	Varaha	Boar	God incarnated as a gigantic boar to rescue the earth from the primordial waters.
4	Narasimha	Man-lion	God incarnated as a half man and half lion (*nara* means man and *simha* means lion) to kill the great demon Hiranyakasipu and rescue his son Prahlad, who was a devotee of God.
5	Vamana	Dwarf	God incarnated as a dwarf to rescue the world from an Asura king named Mahabali.
6	Parasurama	Warrior	God incarnated as a warrior to control the atrocities of Kshatriyas, the warrior race.
7	Rama	House-holder	God incarnated as Lord Rama to kill demons like Ravana and his family.
8	Krishna		God incarnated as Lord Krishna to kill many demons, including the Kauravas.
9	Buddha		God incarnated as Lord Buddha to reform many things in Hinduism (such as animal sacrifice and Brahminism), as well as to teach people an easy way to attain Nirvana.
10	Kalki	Man on the white horse	Kalki will come to eradicate all of creation so that the process of recreation can be started all over again. Kalki will come 427,000 years from now.

Other minor avatars of Lord Vishnu include:
1) Sanat Kumar
2) Sage Narada
3) Saints Nara and Naryana
4) Sage Kapila (founder of Sankya)

5) Dattatreya
6) Yatnya (sacrifice)
7) Rishabha, the first Tirthankara of the Jain religion
8) King Prithu
9) Dhanvatari, the founder of Ayurveda
10) Balarama, the brother of Lord Krishna
11) Sage Veda Vyasa
12) Mohini, the enchantress who deprived the demons of the divine elixir Amruth

Do you think that the Dasa Avatars are related to Charles Darwin's theory of evolution?

It is true that the order of the Dasa Avatars tallies with Darwin's theory of evolution. First Lord Vishnu came as a fish, then as a tortoise, then as a boar, then as a man-lion, then as a boy, a man, and so on. Did early Hindu theologians know about Darwin's theory? Or was Darwin influenced by Hindu concepts, since much of the Platonic thinking underlying Darwin's ideas is of Hindu origin?

Another possibility is that the Hindu rishis might have written with in-depth knowledge about the development of human beings within the womb, where the foetus undergoes a transformation in tune with Darwin's theory of evolution. One theory, put forward by Ernst Haeckel in 1860, states that the embryo of a fish, the embryo of a pig, and the embryo of a human being are all exactly alike. Only a timely transformation makes one a fish, another a pig, and another a human being. (Of course, this theory is disputed by many.)

Lord Krishna said:

"Whenever there is a decay in dharma (righteousness) and outbreak of adharma (non-righteousness). I descend myself for the protection of the good and to annihilate the wicked and for the re-establishment of dharma (righteousness).

I am born from age to age."

(4:7,8)

The incarnations of God are not limited to India. That happens worldwide. When Jewish society had problems, God incarnated as Jesus Christ.

Chapter 23

What is sin?

Details	Verse
Arjuna mentions sin.	1:36
Arjuna will not incur sin.	2:38
Sin is if you give up your duty.	2:33
Why do people sin?	3:36–38, 43
Even if you are the worst sinner in the world.	4:36
Knowledge (jnana) will burn all "karmic debt" to ashes.	4:37
God does not accept sin.	5:15
A person who knows me as the unborn.	10:3

Grandson: What did Lord Krishna say about sin?

Grandfather: Arjuna uses the word paap a few times during the first chapter of the Bhagavad Gita. Lord Krishna also uses the word elsewhere in the Bhagavad Gita.

In Christianity, the idea of sin is based on the "Original Sin" committed by Adam and Eve in the Garden of Eden by eating the forbidden fruit of the Tree of Knowledge of Good and Evil against the commandments of God.

According to that concept, all people, including the newly born, inherit sin from Adam and Eve. All of humanity is punished forever because Adam and Eve ate the forbidden fruit. Christians believe we can have redemption from sin only by accepting Jesus Christ as the Lord and Savior.

Judaism (the mother religion of Christianity) does not believe in the doctrine of "Original Sin" preached by Christians. Likewise, there is no concept of "Original Sin" in Hinduism. Lord Krishna defines sin as selfish thoughts and actions due to ignorance of the natural laws of the universe. Sin in Hinduism is defined as either avoiding one's duty (svadharma) or ignoring injustice (adharma) done against you or against someone else. Hindu scriptures state that one reaps what one sows, whether this is good or bad.

No Hindu will ever say "I am a sinner." The word sinner can only mean someone who makes mistakes due to ignorance (Avidhya), and knowledge (jnana) eradicates ignorance. It is ignorance of natural laws that makes people have improper thoughts and commit wrong actions. Once a person achieves true knowledge, he or she will not commit the same mistake. That is the reason why Hindu scriptures state: "Ignorance is the root of all evils, and knowledge eradicates ignorance."

Hindu scriptures state: "Ignorance is the root of all evils and knowledge eradicates ignorance."
A child puts his hands in fire due to ignorance.
Fire burns the child's hands as per the natural law.
The child gets the knowledge that "fire burns" by his foolish action.
Thereafter, the child will never put his hands in fire.
That example is applicable to everything we think or do in our daily lives.

No one is eternally doomed in Hinduism. Salvation is for all, for the best among us as well as for the worst among us. People make mistakes, and from those mistakes they learn and slowly mature physically, mentally, and spiritually.

At the very beginning of the Bhagavad Gita, Arjuna was

worried that he would inherit sin if he fought and killed all of his relatives in the battle (1:36). But Lord Krishna said to Arjuna that he would not incur any sin if he fights the war, since as a Kshatriya (warrior caste), it is his personal duty (svadharma) to defend his family and eradicate adharma (2:38).

> Lord Krishna said:
> "Even if you are the worst sinner in the world, you can cross over the ocean of sin with a bark of wisdom (jnana)."
> (4:36)

When we attain jnana (true knowledge), sin will automatically vanish, and we will attain self-realization.

> Lord Krishna said:
> "Arjuna, as the blazing fire burns wood to ashes, so does the fire of true knowledge (jnana) burn all karmic debt to ashes."
> (4:37)

Lord Krishna tells us that we will derive no karmic debt if we act selflessly (Nishkama Karma) or surrender all of our actions to God.

> Lord Krishna said:
> "One who does selfless actions, one who performs his duty without attachment, surrendering his actions to God, is not stained or infected by evil, as the lotus leaf is untouched by water."
> (5:10)

Christianity states that sin is the crime against the laws of God, and that God is constantly watching us to make sure we do not break any of his laws. In the Bhagavad Gita, Lord Krishna states that God is not in charge of anyone's activities, whether those activities are sinful or pious. Each one of us has all the freedom in the world to do whatever we want. Lord Krishna did not even try to influence Arjuna's free will. Arjuna had the right to accept everything Lord Krishna taught, as well the right to ignore everything Lord Krishna taught.

> Lord Krishna said:
> "God does not decide the karma each one of us should do, nor does he induce people to act, nor does he create the fruits of any action. Each person acts according to his Vasanas (past and present perceptions of mind).
> God is not responsible for anyone's sinful activities or pious activities. People are mistaken about this since their knowledge is covered by ignorance."
> (5:14–15)

> Lord Krishna said:
> "A person who knows me as someone unborn, without beginning, and the great Lord of the world, is freed from all sins."
> (10:3)

> Lord Krishna said:
> "It is better to perform one's own predetermined duty (svadharma), even if one performs that duty imperfectly, than perform the duty of another (parodharma). When one performs his own predetermined duty in accordance with one's nature, one does not incur any sin."
> (18:47)

Lord Krishna said:
"Even if you are the worst
sinner in the world,
you can cross over the
ocean of sin with
a bark of wisdom (jnana)."
(4:36)

No Hindu will ever say "I am a sinner", since the word sinner only applies to those who make mistakes due to (avidhya). Knowledge (jnana) eradicates ignorance.

Lord Krishna said:
"Arjuna, as the blazing fire
burns wood to ashes,
so does the fire of
knowledge (jnana) burn all
karmic debt to ashes."
(4:37)

Hindu scriptures state:
"Ignorance is the root cause of all evils and
knowledge eradicates ignorance."
A child puts his hand in fire due to his ignorance.
Fire burns the child's hand since that is what fire
always does. The child gets the knowledge (jnana)
that fire burns flesh. Thereafter the child will
never put his hand in fire again. This example is
applicable to everything we think or do in our day-
to-day lives. We learn from the mistakes we make.

Chapter 24

What is Atman?

Details	Verse
Atman (soul) is eternal.	2:16–21
Atman changes bodies like a body changes clothes.	2:22
Weapons cannot cut Atman.	2:23–30
One who takes pleasure in Atman.	3:17–18
The mind is a friend of Atman as well its enemy.	6:5
I am the Atman seated in all beings.	10:20
Atman lives within the body but is unattached.	13:32
Atman does not mix with the body.	13:33
Atman and the gunas.	15:10

Grandson: What is Atman, and why did Lord Krishna give it so much importance?

Grandfather: The Hindu scriptures state that our body is perishable and temporary, and that the soul within the body is immortal. The immortal soul within the body is known as Atman, as well as Jivatman. God is known as Paramatman in the Hindu scriptures.

The earliest use of the word Atman came from the Rig Veda, and the concept was developed in the Upanishads. The Brihadaranyaka Upanishad states that Atman is indeed Brahman (God).

The Katha Upanishad states: "As the one fire, after it has entered the world, takes different forms according to whatever it burns, so does Atman (immortal soul) of all living beings take different forms according to the bodies it enters."

The Upanishads describe Atman as "Neti Neti", meaning, "Not this, not this". By stating that "this is not Atman," "that is not Atman," a jnani (learned person) negates identification with all things of this world which are not the Atman.

The legendary Greek philosophers Aristotle, Plato, and Socrates believed in the immortality of the soul, and they also believed that the soul is invisible and divine. You can read Plato's views on the immortality of the soul in his books called *Republic* and *Phaedo*.

According to the Hindu scriptures, salvation is the process by which a person realizes that he or she is not the perishable body but the Atman—the immortal soul within. That is why Hindu salvation is known as self–realization. Self-realization means "realizing" that one is the "self" (the immortal soul).

Adi Sankara wrote *Atma Shatakam* or *Nirvana Shatakam*, which consists of six verses that tell the world there is only God, and that you and I are indeed that God. His famous poem starts with the verse: "I am neither mind nor intelligence nor ego; I am neither the organs of hearing, nor that of tasting, nor that of smelling, nor that of seeing; I am neither the Sky, nor the Earth, nor the Fire, nor the Air; I am the ever Pure Blissful Consciousness, I am Shiva."

Rishi Yajnavalkya describes Atman in the following manner in the Brihadaranyaka Upanishad:

You cannot see that which the seer of seeing is;
You cannot hear that which the hearer of hearing is;
You cannot think of that which is the thinker of thought;
You cannot know that which the knower of knowledge is.
This is your self that is within everything;
What is other than this is suffering.

Comparing Hindu concepts of salvation with Abrahamic religions like Judaism and Christianity is like comparing apples and oranges. Hindu concepts about salvation are based on the immortality of the soul. In part, this means that heaven and hell are only temporary abodes for the soul, rather than permanent "resting places". Whereas in Abrahamic religions like Judaism and Christianity, there is only one life, after which a person's soul ends up in heaven or hell eternally.

> Lord Krishna said:
> "This self or soul known as Atman is eternal. The body is transitory, and it undergoes changes. Those who are seers of the truth concluded that we are not this perishable material body, but the Atman, the immortal soul."
> (2:16)

Lord Krishna tells us that our physical body is subjected to birth, growth, maturity, reproduction, decay, and death, whereas the self (Atman) is eternal, indestructible, pure, unique, all-knowing, unchangeable, immutable, and inexplicable.

> Lord Krishna continued:
>
> "Arjuna, that which pervades the entire body and mind is indestructible. Nobody can destroy the imperishable soul or Atman.
>
> The physical body inhabited by Atman is mortal. Therefore, as a warrior, you must fight, Oh Arjuna.
>
> One who thinks that Atman is a slayer, and one who thinks Atman is slain: both are ignorant because Atman neither slays nor can be slain.

Atman is neither born nor does it ever die. It is unborn, eternal, permanent, and primeval. Atman is not slain when the body is slain.

Arjuna, how can anyone who knows that Atman is indestructible, eternal, and unborn kill anyone or cause anyone to be killed?"

(2:17–21)

The Aitareya Upanishad 1.1.1 states: "In the beginning there was Atman (immortal soul) only, one and without a second."

Death is never considered to be the end of the journey. It is only the end of the perishable body. After that, the immortal soul (Atman) takes another body, and this cycle of birth and death continues until the person attains self-realization.

Lord Krishna said:
"Just as a person puts on new garments after giving up old ones, similarly, the soul (Atman) secures new bodies after giving up old bodies."
(2:22)

Atman is indestructible.

Lord Krishna said:
"Arjuna, no weapon can cut Atman, fire cannot burn it, water cannot make it wet, and the wind cannot make it dry. Atman cannot be cut, burned, wet, or dried.
(2:23)

Soul is eternal, all pervading, changeless, immovable, and primeval. Atman is beyond space and time.
(2:24)
Atman is said to be unexplainable, incomprehensible, and immutable. Knowing Atman as such, Arjuna, you should not grieve for the physical body."
(2:23–25)

Lord Krishna said:
"Some people look upon Atman as a wonder, some describe it as wonderful, and others hear of it as a wonder. Even after hearing about it, very few people know what Atman is.
O Arjuna, Atman that dwells in the body of all beings is eternal and is indestructible. Therefore, you should not grieve for anybody."
(2:29–30)

Death is certain for one who is born, and birth is certain for one who dies. Therefore, there is no reason why you should lament over the inevitable. One should not lament over the death of anybody at all. Any lamentation is due to attachment, and attachment binds the individual soul to the wheel of transmigration.

Lord Krishna said:
"Arjuna, all beings are unmanifest in their beginning.
They are only manifest in their interim state, and they
are unmanifest again at their end. So there is no need for
crying or lamenting."
(2:28)

A self-realized person has nothing to gain by acting and
nothing to lose by not acting.

Lord Krishna said:
"One who takes pleasure in Atman, who is satisfied in
Atman only: that person has no duties to perform.
That man who has attained self-realization has nothing to
gain by acting and nothing to lose by not acting. He also
does not need to depend on any other living being."
(3:17–18)

Atman is a mirror image of God. You and I can be compared
to electricity within the computer, whereas God is the electricity
within the power plants and networks. But essentially, there is no
difference between Atman and God. That is the reason why our
scriptures say: "Searching after God is like a pinch of salt trying
to find the bottom of the ocean: the moment that pinch of salt
touches the surface of the ocean, it becomes part and parcel of
the ocean...Similarly, a person who searches after God will finally
merge with God, or the limited 'I' (Ego) will become the unlimited
'I' (God)."

In *Vivekachudamani*, Adi Sankara wrote: "Brahma Satyam,
Jagat Mithya, and Jivo Brahmaiva naparah," meaning Brahman or
God alone is truth, the world is unreal, and ultimately there is no

There is no mention of immortal soul in the sixty-six books of the Holy Bible. If there is, the Holy Bible will be supporting the theory of reincarnation as well as the Hindu concepts of salvation.

Ezekiel 18.4, 20 states: "...the soul that sins, it shall die."

atthew 10-28 states: "Fear not them which kill he body, but are not able to kill the soul; but her fear him which is able to destroy both soul and body in Hell."

the contrary, "Dead Sea Scrolls", nostic Gospels," and "Kabbalah" sh mysticism) indicate the belief in the immortality of the soul.

difference between Brahman and the individual self.

Lord Krishna said:
"O Arjuna, I am the soul (Atman), seated in the hearts of all beings. I am the beginning, the middle, and the end of all beings."
(10:20)

Atman lives within the body but is not permanently attached to it.

Lord Krishna said:
"Even though this imperishable soul which is transcendental, eternal, and beyond the modes of nature lives within the material body, the soul neither does anything nor is attached to anything.
The all-pervading sky, due to its subtle nature, does not mix with anything. Similarly, Atman does not mix with the body, even though situated in that body."
(13:32–33)

Lord Krishna said:
"For the soul (Atman) there is neither birth nor death any time. The soul is unborn, eternal, everlasting, and primeval. The soul is not slain when the body is slain."
(2:20)

The soul within the body is immortal and indestructible. It is a mirror image of God. It is indeed God.
The immortal soul is equivalent to the electricity within the computer and God is equivalent to the electricity within the network.

Rishi Ashtavakra told King Jan
"O Mighty king, there is no n
to look high for the stars t
answers. They are already
you. Just reach deep withir
and find out all the an

Luke 17:21 (King Jam
"...behold, the kingdom

The most importar
Greek philosopher
mea

What is the meaning of Neti–Neti?

Neti–Neti means "not this-not this" in Sanskrit.

This statement answers the most important question "**Who Am I?**" (Brihadaranyaka Upanishad 2:3:6)

With the aid of this statement, a person negates the identification of himself or herself as the perishable material body and comes to the realization that he/she is indeed the immortal soul within the body (Atman) which is the mirror image of God.

Through this inquiry, a devotee will finally realize he or she is indeed the immortal soul within the body and will say **Aham Brahmasmi** (I am God).

Chapter 25

What is salvation according to Lord Krishna?

Details	Verse
How to avoid rebirth?	5:17
One in a million realizes me.	7:3–4
He who thinks of me at the time of death.	8:5
My devotee never perishes.	9:31
Give up all dharmas and surrender to me.	18:66
He who thinks of me and me alone.	9:22

Grandson: Grandpa, I know Christians believe that one can attain salvation only by surrendering to Jesus Christ and accepting Jesus Christ as a savior. What is Hindu salvation according to Lord Krishna?

Grandfather: What you said is true. Salvation or "being saved" in Christianity means redemption from the power of sin, and Christians believe that Jesus Christ died for our sins and that only through Jesus Christ can the whole of humanity achieve salvation. Jesus was a Jew, and Jews do not believe in what Christians believe. Hindus also do not believe in that.

According to the Hindu scriptures, salvation is for all. Nobody, even those who have nothing to do with Hinduism, is denied salvation. The best among us will attain salvation with one life, and the worst among us will attain salvation through many lives. The only difference between the best and the worst is the time factor.

What are the ways to attain salvation according to Lord Krishna in the Bhagavad Gita?

Lord Krishna said that there are four paths to attain salvation. They are:

Jnana Yoga	Path of knowledge
Karma Yoga	Path of selfless actions
Raja Yoga	Path of breath control and pranayama
Bhakti Yoga	Path of devotion

According to Lord Krishna, salvation is not possible for those who escape from their duties and run away from life. So to attain salvation, we are bound to do our duties. Those who remain within society, unafraid of the burdens of life, and who live a life of sacrifice, fully surrendering to God, will be more qualified for salvation.

> Lord Krishna said:
> "A liberated soul who is a jnani (person of knowledge), who is free from attachment, and who works for the betterment of the world, dissipates all his karma."
> (4:23)

Whenever salvation is mentioned in the Bhagavad Gita, Lord Krishna always ends up saying "merging with God".

The reason is that Hindus believe that when we sincerely seek after God, ultimately we will become part of God. This happens to everyone irrespective of whether one is a Hindu or not.

Hindu scriptures wrote:
"Searching after God, is like a pinch of salt trying to find the bottom of the ocean. The moment that pinch of salt touches the surface of the ocean, it becomes part of the ocean. Similarly, a person who searches after God will finally merge with God or the limited 'I' (Ego) will become the unlimited 'I' (God)".

According to Hinduism, salvation is for all irrespective of whether or not one is a Hindu.

Nobody, even those who have nothing to do with Hinduism, is ever denied salvation.

The best among us will attain salvation after one life. The worst among us will attain salvation after many lives.

Time is the only difference between the worst and the best.

What is salvation according to Hinduism?

According to Hindu scriptures, man's problem is due to his false belief that he is the perishable material body.

So Hindu salvation is the process by which a person realizes that he or she is not the perishable body but the Atman (the immortal soul within the body).

That is the reason why Hindu salvation is known as **self-realization**. Meaning the realization that one is indeed the self or the immortal soul within the body.
Hindu salvation is also known as **moksha** or **mukti,** meaning liberation or release from the cycles of repeated births and deaths known as samsara.

How can someone attain salvation?

There are four paths or yogas to attain salvation or self-realization. Most people follow **Bhakti Yoga,** the path of total surrender to God.

Jnana Yoga	The path of jnana (knowledge) through introspection and contemplation
Karma Yoga	The path of selfless service by thoughts and actions
Raja Yoga	The path of pranayama and breathing exercises
Bhakti Yoga	The path of total surrender to God

Hindu concepts of salvation
and the salvation concepts
of Abrahamic religions like
Judaism and Christianity
are totally different.

Hindu concepts of salvation are based on
the immortality of the soul as well as on the
reincarnation of the soul, whereas there is no
mention of the immortal soul in the Holy Bible.

The word "immortal" is used in the Holy Bible to
refer to one of God's (not man's) attributes. After
death, a person either goes to heaven or hell
permanently.

Chapter 26

What does Lord Krishna say about the caste system?

Details	Verse
Castes made according to character	4:13
A learned man sees everyone the same	5:18
Sudras	9:31
Karmas associated with castes	18:41–44

Grandson: Grandpa, I am sick and tired of people mentioning caste wherever I go. How can anyone segregate and humiliate people based on the color of their skin, or based on their profession? It is a disgrace and a cancer of our culture.

Grandfather: I fully understand and appreciate your very strong sentiments against the caste system. I agree with them.

But you should also know that this "division of human beings according to vocation" was created during ancient times. When people left their nomadic life style of running around all over the world and settled on the river banks, they started cultivation and family life. At the time when the Rig Veda was written, Indian society was taking roots on the banks of the Indus and Ganges rivers. In order to ensure the smooth functioning of the new society, people were forced to develop some social system. So the caste system was developed with good intentions, in order to precisely divide people according to the work they do.

Later, the caste system degenerated, and human beings were

humiliated and ridiculed according to the color of their skin, as well as their profession. This happened in every society.

For example, the Holy Bible discusses slavery. In the book *Epistle to Philemon*, written by St Paul, St Paul urges a runaway slave called Onesimus to go back to his master Philemon.

Columbus, a very devout Christian and missionary, did not feel any remorse in making American Indians into slaves. The Spanish had no problem in making the Mayans into slaves.

During the US Civil War, Biblical passages were used by over 200 preachers to justify slavery, and Jefferson Davis, President of the Confederate States of America, said that slavery had been established by the decree of Almighty God, that it had been sanctioned in both Testaments of the Bible, from Genesis to Revelation.

In 1999, the Southern Baptist Convention apologized to African Americans for slavery. I congratulate the Christians for giving up on slavery. Likewise, we Hindus have to give up on the caste system.

Lord Krishna, as well as great philosophers like Adi Sankara, have stated repeatedly that caste is based on aptitude (guna) and vocation, independent of sex, birth, or breeding.

Here is what Lord Krishna said to Arjuna in the Bhagavad Gita about the caste system. Lord Krishna said that he himself had created the caste system according to people's natural attributes and aptitudes, based on the gunas and karma. The four castes—the Brahmin, the Kshatriya, the Vaishya, and the Sudra—are like the four limbs of the human body. It is said that the Brahmins are born from the head of the Lord, the Kshatriyas from the shoulders, the Vaishyas from the thighs, and the Sudras from the feet.

The Rig Vedic hymn known as Purusha Sukta states: "The Brahmin was Purusha's (cosmic man's) mouth, the Kshatriya his arms, the Vaishya his thighs, and the Sudra his feet." (Rig Veda 10:19:11–12)

Just as each limb is important and has a function of its own, but interdependent, so too, all these castes are equally important. Further, by virtue of the gunas each individual possesses, they can transcend their castes.

Lord Krishna said:
"According to people's born aptitudes (gunas) and professional interests, I created the four divisions called varna, or caste, of human society. Even though I am the author of the caste system, one should know that I do nothing and I am eternal."
(4:13)

Lord Krishna further said:
"A learned and enlightened person sees with equal vision a learned Brahmin, an outcast, a cow, an elephant, or a dog."
(5:18)

In the Mahabharata, in the very popular dialog between Yaksha and Dharmaputra, Yaksha tells Dharmaputra: "A man does not become a Brahmin by the mere fact of his birth, not even by the acquisition of Vedic scholarship; it is good character alone that can make one a Brahmin. He will be worse than a Sudra if his conduct is not in conformity with the rules of good behaviour."

As I said before, the concept of gunas originated in the Sankhya philosophy. The three gunas are sattva (goodness, construction, harmony), rajas (passion, activity, confusion), and tamas (darkness, destruction, chaos). All of these three gunas are present in everyone, but each of us has a different proportion of gunas. The interplay of these three gunas defines a person's character and determines the progress of life.

Lord Krishna said:
"Nobody born on earth can exist independent of the three gunas born of material nature.

O Arjuna, duties of Brahmins, Kshatriyas, Vaishyas, and Sudras are classified in accordance with the gunas they are born with or according to their natures.

Honesty, knowledge, wisdom, tranquillity, self-control, austerity, purity, forgiveness, and faith in God are the natural qualities of a Brahmin.

Heroism, power, determination, resourcefulness, courage, generosity, and leadership are the natural qualities of a Kshatriya.

Arjuna, those who have skills in farming, taking care of cattle, business, trade, and so on are known as Vaishyas. Those who merely do service and labor are classified as Sudras.

When one is devoted to one's own duty, one attains perfection. Please listen as I explain further how a person can find perfection through his duties (svadharma).

A human being can attain perfection by worshipping God through his actions, for duties of life come from God, who presides over all things.

Performing one's own inborn duty (svadharma) is better than performing the duty of another faultlessly. When one performs one's own inborn duty, one does not incur any evil."

(18:40–47)

The most popular and legendary author Rishi Veda Vyasa was the son of Satyavati, a low caste fisherwoman. Sage Valmiki, the author of the Ramayana, was a low caste hunter. Sage Aitareya, who wrote the Aitareya Upanishad, was born of a Sudra woman. Sage Vidura, who was the religious advisor of King Dhritarashtra, was born to a low caste woman servant of the palace. So the idea that every low caste person ought to be ill-treated is equally wrong.

Adi Sankara, even though a Brahmin, condemned caste and meaningless ritual as foolish. He said that every human being takes birth as a Sudra. Only by education and upbringing can he or she become "twice born" into a higher caste.

"Untouchability" is still a curse on Hinduism. One great untouchable who became a prominent leader of modern India, B.R. Ambedker, wrote: "To the untouchables, Hinduism is a veritable chamber of horrors."

Mahatma Gandhi said: "Untouchability is a crime against God and men." Gandhi addressed the untouchables by the name Harijans, meaning "children of God". He fought for their emancipation, and in 1949, soon after independence from Britain, the government of India made it a criminal offence to persecute "untouchables".

Still, in many parts of India, you can come across ugly relics of the caste system.

The caste system is a disgrace. It is a cancer and it should be eradicated for the good of India.

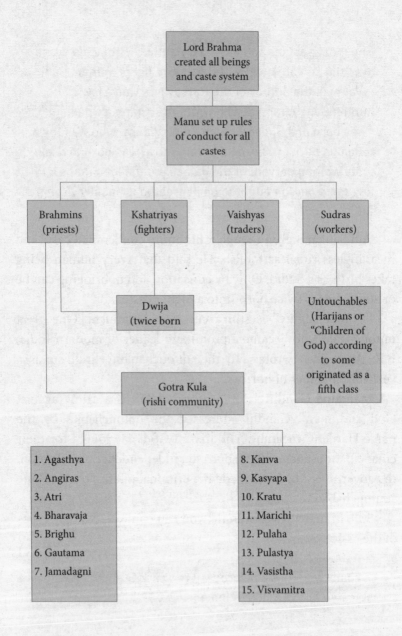

Lord Krishna said:

"Arjuna, according to people's born aptitudes (gunas) and professional interests, I created the four divisions called varnas or castes of human society. Even though I am the author of the caste system, I am not responsible for the good and bad results of it. One should know that I do nothing and I am eternal."

(4:13)

Caste is based on aptitude (guna) and vocation. It is independent of sex, birth, or breeding.

Lord Krishna further said
about caste:

"A learned and enlightened
person sees with equal vision a
learned Brahmin, an outcast, a
cow, an elephant, or a dog."
(5:18)

Adi Sankara, even though a Brahmin, condemned caste and meaningless rituals as foolish. He said every human being takes birth as a Sudra. Only by education and upbringing does he or she become a "twice born" (Dwija).

In the Mahabharata, in the very popular dialogue between Yaksha and Dharmaputra, Yaksha tells Dharmaputra:

"A man does not become a Brahmin by the mere fact of his birth, not even by the acquisition of Vedic scholarship; it is good character alone that can make one a Brahmin. He will be worse than a Sudra if his conduct is not in conformity with the rules of good behavior."

The caste system is still a major problem in India.

The country that gave us the Vedas and Upanishads should be sad that the caste system still prevails in India.

India will not be free until every Dalit girl or boy can walk with his or her head high and proudly say, "I am a Hindu."

Who are Dalits?
They are the oppressed or outcaste people of Hinduism, previously known as untouchables.

Chapter 27

Why do bad things happen to good people?

Details	Verse
God does not make karmas, only nature does.	5:14
God does not accept paap (sin) or punya.	5:15
Why do people sin?	3:36–43

Grandson: Why do bad things happen to good people?

Grandfather: Why bad things happen to good people is an excellent question.

As Lord Krishna pointed out in the Bhagavad Gita, good and bad things happen to people according to their accumulated karmic debt. Sometimes that karmic debt may be due to the karma done in this life, but many times it was acquired during previous lives. God has given us absolute freedom of thoughts and actions, and what we do with that freedom is left to each one of us.

Lord Krishna said:
"God does not decide the karma each one of us should do, nor does he induce people to act, nor does he create the fruits of any action. Each person acts according to his vasanas (past and present perceptions of mind).
God is not responsible for anyone's sinful activities or pious activities. People are mistaken about this since their knowledge is covered by ignorance."
(5:14–15)

Before you ask God,
"I want to be just like him or her,"
please ask yourself what you are
asking God.

Sometimes the pretty girl whom you
are jealous of, whom the world adores,
may be suffering from all kinds of
diseases, or may be a drug addict or
may be a victim of spousal abuse.

So God will laugh at you if you beg God
to make you just like her.

Comparing one's life with everyone else's will only bring forth misery. Jealousy and depression will take over us when we believe the myth that the grass is always greener on the other side of the fence.

Chapter 28

Who is an enlightened person?

Details	Verse
Arjuna asks about the signs of an enlightened person.	2:54
Lord Krishna explains Sthita Prajna (enlightened person).	2:55 to 57

Grandson: What is a Sthita Prajna?
Grandfather: A Sthita Prajna is a person who lives in the world like all of us, but nothing in the world affects him or her. A Sthita Prajna sees the presence of God in everything. He or she is not affected by dualities such as cold or hot, happiness or unhappiness. The Sthita Prajna is not bound by the laws or traditions of society, nor by the injunctions of the scriptures.

There are thousands, if not millions in the world who are Sthita Prajna, yet who have nothing to do with Hinduism or who have not read any verse in the Bhagavad Gita. To say you have to be a Hindu to become a Sthita Prajna does not make any sense at all. An enlightened person can come in many forms and shapes in any nation on earth.

A Sthita Prajna is humble, happy, peaceful, emotionally stable, loving, kind, spiritual, and compassionate. They will be egoless and will avoid all publicity, serving the world in complete obscurity.

Lord Krishna answered:
"When a person has renounced all desires of the mind and finds satisfaction in the self alone, then he is said to be in pure transcendental consciousness, and he is called an enlightened person named Sthita Prajna.

In suffering as well as in happiness, his mind is neither deluded nor delighted. That person, who is completely free from attachment, fear, and anger, is called Sthita Prajna. One who is not attached to anything, free from all material affection, who is neither thrilled by getting desired results nor disturbed by undesired results, his intellect is considered steady."

(2:55–57)

Purusharthas

The four aims of life were developed by the rishis to help a human being to mature slowly from materialism to spirituality.

Purusharthas do not mean a life of negation but a very balanced life.

The four purusharthas are:

1.	Dharma (duty, righteousness)
2.	Artha (wealth)
3.	Kama (desire, passion)
4.	Moksha (salvation or liberation)

Chapter 29
What does Lord Krishna say about birth, death, and reincarnation?

Details	Verse
The wise grieve neither for the living nor for the dead.	2:11:12
Atman experiences changes in the body, from youth to old age.	2:13
Atman is neither born, nor does it die, nor cease to exist.	2:20
Atman acquires new bodies after discarding old worn-out bodies just like the body changing clothes.	2:22
Birth and death are unavoidable.	2:27
All beings are not noticeable before birth and after death.	2:28
After many incarnations (births and deaths), a person surrenders to me.	7:19
Thoughts at the time of death	8:5–6
Time of death	8:23
Best time to die	8:24
Bad time to die	8:25
There are two ways of departing from the world. One is light and another is darkness.	8:26

Grandson: As far as I know, some religions like Christianity only believe in one life and do not believe in reincarnation at all. They believe that after death a person either ends up in heaven or hell for eternity. What did Lord Krishna say about birth, death, and reincarnation?

Grandfather: What you said is very true. Some religions believe that when a person dies, he or she ends up either in heaven or hell, whereas Hindus believe that heaven and hell are temporary abodes rather than a final destination.

According to Hinduism, salvation means realizing that one is indeed the immortal soul and giving up the false belief that one is the perishable material body. Just like a man discards his old clothes for new ones, so too, the immortal soul within the perishable body leaves the worn-out body and enters a new body at the time of death. Atman migrates from body to body.

> Lord Krishna said that birth and death are part and parcel of life. If one is born, one has to die one day. Nobody escapes from the claws of death.

The immortal soul is guided to a new body by the sum total of karmic debt attached to it. If a person had a very spiritual life, that person will be reborn into a home where he or she can continue their search for truth. If a person led an immoral, vicious life, after death he or she will be born to wicked parents, in whose home he or she can continue his or her wicked life, just as the child of a tennis player will learn to play tennis faster than a child born into an ordinary home.

Right from the very beginning of the Bhagavad Gita, Lord Krishna discusses this subject.

> Lord Krishna said:
> "You are lamenting about those who are not worthy of grief, and yet speak words of wisdom. The wise grieve neither for the living nor for the dead. There was never a time when you, I, or any of these kings did not exist, nor shall there be a time when any of us cease to exist in the future.
> Just as the immortal soul experiences changes in the body, from youth to old age, the immortal soul will acquire another body after death. The wise are not puzzled about this, since they know that is a fact of life."
> (2:11–13)

Lord Krishna said:
"As far as the immortal soul is concerned, there is neither birth nor death at any time. Atman is neither born, nor does it die, nor does it cease to exist. Atman is unborn, eternal, ever-existing, and primeval. Atman is not killed when the body is killed."
(2:20)

Lord Krishna said:
"Just as a person puts on new garments after discarding the old ones, similarly the Atman (immortal soul) acquires new bodies after discarding old worn-out bodies."
(2:22)

Lord Krishna said:
"Arjuna, birth and death are part of life. One who has taken birth is sure to die, and after death one is sure to take birth again. Therefore, you should not lament.

Arjuna, all beings are not noticeable before birth or after death. They are noticeable only between the birth and death interval. So there is no cause to grieve. Once again, birth and death are two sides of the same coin."
(2:27–28)

Lord Krishna said:
"After many incarnations, the person who is aware of the self surrenders to me (God), knowing that I am everything."
(7:19)

> Lord Krishna said:
> "At the time of death, whosoever leaves his body, remembering me alone, attains me. There is absolutely no doubt about this.
> Arjuna, whatever one thinks when he leaves his body, that state he will attain without fail in his next life."
> (8:5–6)

> Lord Krishna said:
> "Arjuna, one who leaves the body while meditating on God (Brahman) and uttering Aum (Om), the sacred monosyllable sound of God (Brahman), attains the supreme goal of merging with God."
> (8:13)

Is it true that Bhishma waited for the Mahabharata War to end so that he could depart from the earth during the Uttarayana, or the six months when the sun travels north?

What you said is very true. Bhishma, the grandfather of both the Kauravas and the Pandavas, waited for the *Uttarayana* (*uttara*, or "north," and *ayana*, or "movement," the six months when the sun travels north) to commence before leaving his body.

Ancient Romans also celebrated the commencement of the beginning of Uttarayana by recognizing the birth of the pagan Sun God, Mithra, on 25 December. Mithra was worshipped throughout the Roman Empire, and later the Romans used the same date to celebrate Christmas as the birthday of Jesus Christ, even though there is no mention of the date of Jesus's birth in the Holy Bible.

> Lord Krishna said:
> "Arjuna, let me explain to you the different times when yogis departing from the world never return.
> Those who know God (Brahman) and depart life during fire, light, bright lunar fortnight, and the six months when the sun travels north will not take birth again.
> Those who depart during smoke, night, the dark lunar fortnight, and the six months when the sun travels south will take birth again.
> According to the Vedas, there are two ways of departing from the world. One is light and another is darkness. Those who die in light will not take birth again, and those who die during darkness will definitely take birth again."
> (8:23–26)

Chapter 30

Is the whole universe only maya, or illusion?

Details	Verse
Maya (illusion), consisting of three gunas, is difficult to overcome.	7:13–14
Through my maya, I create everything.	9:7–8
I am death, devourer of all.	10:34

Grandson: What is Maya?

Grandfather: Maya means "illusion". The word maya is derived from the Sanskrit root words *ma,* meaning "not", and *ya,* meaning "that". So the meaning of maya is "that which is not". (Maya was also the name of the mother of Lord Buddha.)

Hindu scriptures state that the world we perceive and experience is unreal and temporal. God and the immortal soul alone are real and eternal; everything else comes and goes.

Adi Sankara stated that at night, one may easily mistake a rope for a snake. In doing so, one is subjected to confusion and fear. Thus according to him, fear and other emotions are based on illusion, an incorrect perception of reality.

Lord Krishna states that the whole creation is his leela (divine child's play), and that creation came from his maya (illusion). You and I suffer because we are part and parcel of that maya (illusion).

Lord Krishna said:
"Just as a person puts on new garments after discarding the old ones, similarly the immortal soul acquires new bodies after discarding old worn-out bodies." (2:22)

Death is never considered as the end of a journey. It is only the end of the perishable body.

After that the immortal soul takes another body and these cycles of birth and death continue until the person attains self-realization.

Lord Krishna said:

"Just like the immortal soul experiences changes in the body, from youth to old age, the immortal soul will acquire another body after death. The wise are not puzzled about this since they know that it is a fact of life."

(2:13)

Atman takes birth again and again until the body exhausts all karmic debt. This is cyclical and prepetual and it happens in every person's life, whether he or she is a Hindu or not.

Lord Krishna said:

"As the fire is covered by smoke, as a mirror is covered by dust, and as an embryo is covered by the womb, so too one's proper understanding of the truth (jnana) is covered by passion."

(3:38)

Jnana (knowledge) is not bookish or intellectual knowledge. One can attain jnana only though the eradication of the ego. Jnana is knowledge through experience.

> Lord Krishna said:
> "O Arjuna, in the beginning of time (Kalpa), through my maya, I create everything, and at the end of time, the whole creation merges in me. By my will the whole universe is created and annihilated again and again."
> (9:7–8)

Lord Krishna also warns us that his maya (illusion) is so powerful that it is not easy to transcend it. Under the influence of the three gunas, a person is misled and subsequently entangled and entrapped.

Further, under the very powerful influence of maya, people mistakenly identify themselves with their perishable material bodies. Only by surrendering to the will of God can one transcend this maya.

> Lord Krishna said:
> "Being deluded by three gunas, the entire universe does not recognize God, who is above the mind and is imperishable. My maya, consisting of three gunas, is difficult to overcome. But those who have surrendered themselves to me can easily cross beyond my illusion."
> (7:13–14)

In the Srimad Bhagavatam Purana, it is written: "One God has become many through his maya." The Brihadaranyaka Upanishad states that God takes many forms through his maya.

God alone exists, and everything else is maya.

> Stressing the cyclical nature of creation and destruction, Lord Krishna said:
> "I am life, cause of all life, and I am death, devourer of all."
> (10:34)

This whole process of perpetual creation and annihilation of the universe is known as leela, meaning "child's play of God." When God incarnates on earth, it is called leela manusha vigraha, or God assuming the human body as a leela.

Lord Krishna is telling us that pursuing happiness in a material world is like pursuing the mirage of an oasis in the desert, since one will never find water in a desert. Similarly, the material world provides no real happiness, which exists only as an elusive dream.

> Just as the "on" and "off" switches in a network make thousands of forms of "illusion" for all of us, through maya, God is creating all of the illusion again and again.

Lord Krishna is telling us that one can only transcend maya by realizing that one is the immortal soul (Atman) within the body. That is the reason why Hindu salvation is known as self-realization. That is also the reason, as I have said, why our scriptures say that sin is only ignorance of the truth, and that jnana (knowledge) eradicates ignorance.

Now I am confused. If the whole creation is an illusion, why should I do anything?

Excellent question. Even Arjuna had the same question. The only answer is as follows: As long as we see the material world as real, we are forced to act as if it's real until we can achieve Advaita perception and see only the immortal soul and God as real. In other words: if you suspect that something is a snake, you have to take all precautions to handle it properly, even if later you find out that the thing you suspected was a snake was actually a rope.

Thus neither Arjuna nor any one of us can run away and live a lazy life. All of us are forced to adhere to the appropriate dharmas for each stage in our life until we attain salvation.

What is Maya?

Maya means "illusion". The word maya is derived from the Sanskrit root words *ma* meaning not and *va* meaning that. So the meaning of maya is that which is not.

Hindu scriptures state that the world we perceive and experience is unreal and God alone is real. Everything else comes and goes. God and the immortal soul within the body are real and eternal. All matter is unreal and temporal.

In *Vivekachudamani*,
Adi Sankara wrote:

"Brahma Satyam,
Jagat Mithya,
Jivo Brahmaiva naparah"
meaning
Brahman or God alone is truth, the
world is unreal, and ultimately there
no difference between Brahman
(God) and the individual self
(Atman).

God and Atman are the same. God is the
electricity within the network and Atman is the
electricity within the computer. That is the reason
why all realized persons will always say Aham
Brahmasmi (I am God).

Chapter 31

How can a person control his thoughts and mind?

Details	Verse
When a person constantly thinks about objects	2:62–63
Those who have control over the mind	6:6–7
Drawing back the mind	6:26
The difficulty of controlling the mind	6:34–6

Grandson: How can a person control his thoughts and mind?

Grandfather: The Bhagavad Gita deals with the mind in a very detailed manner, especially in its sixth chapter. According to Lord Krishna, the problems human beings experience are due to scattered, random, and half-organized thoughts, and he tells Arjuna different methods to control the mind.

Lord Krishna first analyzes our problems like a psychiatrist:

> Lord Krishna said:
> "When a person constantly thinks about objects, attachment for those objects arises in the mind. From attachment, desire is born, and from desire, anger is born. From anger comes delusion, from delusion comes loss of memory, from loss of memory comes destruction of the intellect, and once the intellect is destroyed, the person perishes.
> (2:62–63)

Throughout the Bhagavad Gita, Lord Krishna tells us that if we can become the masters of our thoughts, we can become the masters of our lives, as well as the masters of the world around us.

According to a very popular health magazine, an ordinary person has over 30,000 thoughts a day. So when we do not control our thoughts, we create conditions for all kinds of illness. Fear itself triggers more than 1,400 known physical and chemical responses, which means that toxic thoughts may cause illnesses such as diabetes, cancer, or asthma, to name just a few. So we are forced to consciously control our thoughts.

One of the best books about the mind is *Think and Grow Rich* by Napoleon Hill. It is one of the classic books that every person should read in his or her lifetime.

> Lord Krishna said:
> "To those who have control over the mind, the mind is a friend; but for those who have no control over the mind, the mind acts like an enemy.
> (6:6)

If you can become the master of your thoughts, you can become the master of your life, as well as the master of the world around you. The Maitri Upanishad states that the "mind can be the source of bondage, or can be the source of liberation."

> Lord Buddha said:
> "Your worst enemy cannot harm you as much as your own unguarded thoughts."

We have to develop a mind which is open to everything and at the same time attached to nothing. That is what Lord Krishna is teaching us in the Bhagavad Gita.

> Lord Krishna said:
> "One who can control the mind and attain tranquillity,
> to that man heat and cold, pleasure and pain, honor and
> dishonor are the same."
> (6:7)

Knowing the power of the mind and its capability to wander, Lord Krishna asks us to constantly watch it. Like a turtle withdrawing its limbs when it sees danger, we should withdraw our mind and keep it under the control of the self all the time.

> Lord Krishna said:
> "Whenever the mind goes unsteady and wanders, one must
> draw it back and keep it under the control of the self."
> (6:26)

At this point, Arjuna tells Lord Krishna that the mind is unsteady, turbulent, powerful, and obstinate—and as such, very difficult to control.

> Arjuna said:
> "O Krishna, since the mind is unsteady, turbulent,
> obstinate, and very strong, controlling the mind is more
> difficult than controlling the wind."
> Lord Krishna answered:
> "Arjuna, no doubt the mind is very difficult to control.
> However, it can be controlled by constant practice and
> detachment.

Self-realization is not at all possible for one whose mind is out of control. But for the person who has/his or her mind under control and who tries by appropriate methods of yoga, self-realization is possible."
(6:34–36)

We have to develop an attitude of remaining open to everything while at the same never becoming attached to anything. People who develop that mindset will live an exciting and balanced life.

Lord Krishna said:
"For those who have control
of the mind, the mind is a
friend; but for those who have
no control over the mind,
the mind acts like their
worst enemy." (6:6)

Lord Buddha said:
"The mind is everything
What you think you become."

Lord Krishna said:

"One who can control the mind and attain tranquillity, to that man heat and cold, pleasure and pain, honor and dishonor are the same."
(6:7)

Knowing the power of the mind and its capability to wander. Lord Krishna asks us to constantly watch it.
Like a turtle withdrawing its limbs on seeing danger, we should draw back our mind and keep it under control all the time.

Chapter 32

Who or what is God?

Details	Verse
Whenever there is a decline in dharma and rise of adharma	4:7–8
He who sees Me (God) everywhere and sees everything in Me	6:30
Brahman and human form	9:11
Qualities of God	9:16–19
How Brahman manifests	13:18
How one understands Brahman	13:29

Grandson: Grandfather, I have learnt in my class that in Christianity, God is described as a Trinity: God the Father, God the Son, and God the Holy Ghost. How is God described in the Bhagavad Gita?

Grandfather: It is true that in Christianity, God has been described as a Trinity since the very first Christian council meeting at Nicaea in 325 CE. There is still no word such as Trinity in the Holy Bible.

Hindus have no problem seeing Jesus Christ as an incarnation of God. Jesus was a Jew, but Jews do not believe in the Trinity.

As you may know, there are thirty-three Hindu gods in the Rig Veda, and in fact there are hundreds of gods besides these. But during the time of the Rig Veda, out of all those gods emerged Brahman, the one and only God, which expresses itself in trillions of forms and trillions of names. Brahman is also described as a Trinity (Brahma—God of Creation; Vishnu—God of Preservation; Shiva—God of Annihilation).

God is not a man or a woman.
In fact, nobody knows what God is.
That is the reason why God is described as "it" in Hindu scriptures.
God or Brahman is described as "it" and is the infinite, eternal, indescribable, omniscient, pervasive, genderless, eternal truth and bliss which does not change, yet is the cause of all changes.
Brahman is without any beginning and any end. The Upanishads describe Brahman as one and indivisible, the eternal universal self who is present in all.

The Bhagavad Gita, like all other scriptures, describes Brahman in vivid details. As we have discussed, by showing Arjuna his Viswaroopa (formless form), Lord Krishna proved to the whole world that he is indeed the personification of God, the Brahman.

In *Vivekachudamani*, Adi Sankara wrote that: "Brahman alone is Truth, the world is unreal, and ultimately there is no difference between Brahman and Atman."
"God is everything, everything is God"—this is the basis of the Advaita philosophy.

The Hindu scriptures describe Brahman in two ways:

Saguna Brahman	God with attributes	Viswaroopa
Nirguna Brahman	God without attributes	God as described in the Upanishads

This parallels the Old Testament of the Bible. In Exodus, when Moses asked God, "Who are you?" the answer came from the burning bushes: "I am what I am." Thus the Hebrew God, like Nirguna Brahman, is not a being with human attributes.

From Brahman originated Aum. Aum is the vibration of God from which all of creation emerged.

As a rule, the rest of the religions in the world killed people who worshipped other gods than their chosen God. They always say that their God is the only true God, and that other gods of other religions are false gods.

In Hinduism, the rishis allowed everyone to worship God in any form with any name one wants. This is allowed based on the concept: "When you worship any god, you are actually worshipping the One and Only God, Brahman."

Apart from that, all of the Hindu scriptures, including the Bhagavad Gita, teach us that God is within us. So do not look elsewhere for God, but within each one of us.

Rishi Vasistha told Lord Rama in Yoga Vasistha:
"You are Brahman, I am Brahman, and the whole universe is Brahman. Whatever you are doing, realize this truth at all times. This Brahman or the self alone is the reality in all beings, even as clay is the real substance in thousands of pots."

Remember the quote about how searching for God is like a pinch of salt trying to find the bottom of the ocean. Lord Krishna describes the same concept in the following verse:

Lord Krishna said:
"Arjuna, he who sees Me (God) everywhere and sees everything in Me, I am never lost to him, nor is he ever lost to Me."
(6:30)

> Lord Krishna said:
> "Fools ridicule me since I took the human form, not understanding my mystical nature as the Lord of all beings, the Brahman itself."
> (9:11)

> Lord Krishna said:
> "I am the ritual; I am the sacrifice, and the offering. I am the medicine, the mantra, the offering to the ancestors. I am the butter and the fire and the offering.
> I am the father of this universe, its mother, and the grandfather. I am knowledge (jnana) and the syllable Aum. I am also the Rig, the Sama, and the Yajur Vedas.
> Arjuna, I am everything. I radiate heat, and I withhold and send forth rain. I am immortality as well as death. I am what you see as well as what you do not see. Both that which exists and that which does not exist is I.
> I am the supreme goal, sustainer, Lord, witness, abode, refuge, and friend. I am the creation and the annihilation, the basis of everything, the resting place, and I am the imperishable seed."
> (9:16–19)

> Lord Krishna said:
> "One who sees God situated equally everywhere, in every living being, does not degrade himself by his mind. Hence he attains the Brahman."
> (13:29)

God is not a man;
God is not a woman;
Nobody knows what God is.

That is the reason why in many
scriptures
God is referred to as "it".

God did not make man in his image,
Man indeed made God in his own image since
man cannot conceive a nameless and formless
God.

To say "God is a father" or "God is a mother"
is strictly to help a devotee to concentrate on a
nameless, formless God during the initial stages
of his or her devotion.

Hindus worship

the

One and Only

God

Brahman

with trillions of

names and in

trillions of

forms.

Brahman is the absolute God of Hinduism. It is the eternal, infinite, omnipresent, and absolute reality.

Brahman is described in two ways in Hindu scriptures.

From that God, Brahman, originated Aum (Om). Aum is the vibratory aspect of God from which the whole universe emerged.

Saguna Brahman	God with attributes	Such as Viswaroopa
Nirguna Brahman	God without attributes	God described in the Upanishads

Godhead is further divided into Trinity.	
Lord Brahma	God of Creation. This is not a person but a title. One Brahma lives for 311.04 trillion years and after that another Brahma will appear.
Lord Vishnu	God of Preservation
Lord Shiva	God of Annihilation

By worshipping any god, you are actually worshipping the only God, Brahman.

Hindus treat Jesus Christ as an incarnation of God.

Lord Krishna said:
"Whenever there is a decline in dharma (righteousness) and rise of adharma (non-righteousness) I descend myself, for the protection of the good and the destruction of the wicked and for the establishment of righteousness. I come into being from age to age."
(4:7,8)

When Jewish society had problems, God incarnated as Jesus Christ to take care of them.

Chapter 33

What is Aum (Om)?

Details	Verse
Aum and self-realization	8:12, 13
I am the sacred syllable Aum	9:17
Among letters I am the letter *A*	10:17
Om Tat Sat as the representation of truth	17:23
Aum while undertaking rituals	17:24

Grandson: What does Aum mean?

Grandfather: Aum, or Om, is the vibratory aspect of God from which the whole of creation emerged. The sound of Aum is called Anahada Nada in Sanskrit, meaning "unstruck sound", or "sound produced without striking two things together".

Aum is the sound of the universe itself. Aum is the primary mantra (Pranava mantra) in Hinduism. All the cosmos stems from the vibration of the sound Aum.

Lord Krishna addressed the importance of Aum in the life of every human being through many verses in the Bhagavad Gita. Sage Patanjali, the author of the Patanjali Yoga Sutra, wrote: "He who knows Aum knows God."

Aum is mentioned in the Yajur Veda as Pranava—the "humming sound", or the "elevating sound". The Mandukya Upanishad states that Aum symbolizes everything that manifests. The Maitri Upanishad states that Aum is the primordial throb of the universe. It is the sound of the immortal soul, or Atman.

> Lord Krishna said:
> "He who controls all his sense organs, he who fixes his mind on the heart, fixing his vital force at the top of his head, and utters Aum and thinks of me when he quits his body, will attain self-realization."
> (8:12–13)

Everything in the whole universe is vibrating. Everything is vibrating at one frequency or another. The ancient rishis knew that behind everything is a vibration and that this humming vibration is the base of all matter.

Aum is the force behind everything from bacteria to galaxies. Aum should be heard within us. It is not a sound we can make with our vocal chords. However, when we chant Aum, we will eventually start hearing the true Aum within us.

> Lord Krishna said:
> "I am the father of this universe, its mother, and the grandfather. I am knowledge (jnana) and the syllable Aum. I am also the Rig, the Sama, and the Yajur Vedas."
> (9:17)

> Lord Krishna said:
> "Arjuna, these syllables 'Om Tat Sat' are the symbolic threefold representation of the Absolute Truth. These syllables were used by Brahmins while chanting the hymns of the Vedas and during sacrifices.
> Therefore, those who adhere to the Vedas begin with the sacred word Aum (Om) whenever undertaking scripturally prescribed acts of sacrifice, charity, penances.

Without any desire for the fruit of actions, those who desire liberation from the cycles of birth and death (samsara) utter the syllable 'tat' during the acts of sacrifice, penance, and charity.

The word 'Sat' is used to indicate truth and reality. During the performance of all sacred activities the word 'Sat' is also used."
(17:23–26)

There is a very strange connection between the Aum (Om) vibration and the string theory in physics, or the Theory of Everything. According to the M-theory, a variant of the string theory, atoms are made up of vibrating strings. If we compare an atom to the whole solar system, the vibratory strings would only have the size of a small electric bulb. Every aspect of the physical world would be a function of the different frequencies at which these subatomic strings vibrate. These "vibrating strings" throughout the universe, which take various shapes and exist beyond time and space, are what connect the four forces in nature: gravity, electromagnetism, and the strong and weak nuclear forces.

Who knows: could the vibration that binds the universe together be Aum?

Aum is a sacred sound that is considered the greatest of all mantras. It is said that the sound can be produced by ringing a bell, but it can also take the form of a spoken syllable. The syllable Aum is composed of the three sounds a-u-m (in Sanskrit, the vowels "a" and "u" combine to become o), and the symbol's threefold nature is central to its meaning. The visual symbol for Aum consists of three curves, one semicircle, and a dot. The large bottom curve symbolizes the waking state, A. The middle curve signifies the dream state, U. The upper curve denotes the state of deep sleep, M. The dot signifies the fourth state of consciousness, or the Turiya state.

Aum represents several important triads:

	A	U	M
Three states	Waking	Dream	Deep sleep
Three worlds	Earth	Underworld	Heaven
Three gods	Brahma	Vishnu	Shiva
Three Vedas	Rig Veda	Yajur Veda	Sama Veda

The Katha Upanishad states: "The goal, which all Vedas declare, which all austerities aim at, and which humans desire when they live a life of conscience, I will tell you briefly: it is Aum." Speaking of Aum, the Taittiriya Upanishad states: "Thou art the sheath of Brahman." That is, Aum is the container for the Supreme, and to invoke Aum is to invoke the Supreme.

The Mandukya Upanishad is devoted entirely to the meaning and explanation of Aum. It states that Aum stands for the Supreme Reality as a symbol for what was, what is, and what shall be. Aum represents also what lies beyond past, present, and future. It is also a symbolic representation of the various compartments of the psyche and an interdimensional map of the relationship each part of consciousness has to the divine within.

Aum is also the logos, or Word, described in the Bible. John 1:1 states: "In the beginning was the Word, and the Word was with God, and the Word was God." But long before John 1:1 was written, this could be found in the Vedas: "In the beginning was Prajapathi, the Brahman, the God, with whom was the word: And the word was verily the Supreme Brahman—the God."

Aum (Om)
is the vibratory aspect of God from which
the whole of creation emerges.

The sound of Aum is called Anahada Nada in Sanskrit meaning "unstruck sound" or "sound produced without striking two things together".

Everything in the whole universe is vibrating. Everything is vibrating at one frequency or another. Even the human body is made of electronic vibration. The ancient rishis knew that behind everything is a vibration and that humming vibration is the base of all matter.

Aum is the sound of the universe itself. Aum is the primary mantra (Pranava mantra) in Hinduism. All the cosmos stems from the vibration of the sound Aum.

Aum is the force behind everything from bacteria to galaxies. During 2010, for the very first time, astronomers at the University of Sheffield recorded the vibrations produced by the magnetic field in the outer atmosphere of the sun. Some say that the recorded vibrations sound like Aum.

Chapter 34

What does Lord Krishna say about idol worship?

Details	Verse
Krishna and Atman	6:31
Ignorance and idol worship	7:24–25
Worship of Krishna versus Brahman	12:1–5

Grandson: What did Lord Krishna say about idol worship?

Grandfather: Lord Krishna has described with vivid detail what God is and how God is worshipped by devotees. Hindus do not worship idols. Hindus use idols like everyone else to worship God who has no name or form (Nama-roopa). Hindus have no problem calling that God Jehovah, Jesus, Brahman, or other names. God is omnipresent and omniscient, and nobody can monopolize God. Thus Hindus never ever say or believe that an idol is God.

But other religions say that Hindus worship idols.

What are they saying is not true! If someone says that Hindus worship idols, so too, does everybody else. The cross in the church, statues of Virgin Mary, statues of patron saints, pictures and statues of Jesus Christ: they are all idols in the true definition of the word. When the Pharaoh Akhenaten, the father of King Tut, began to worship one God, the Aten, that God was symbolized by the idol of the sun disc.

Neither a Christian nor a Jew will say that they are worshiping an idol. But Hindus are not worshipping idols either. Everyone is using the form of the idol to concentrate on God, who has no form.

God is not a man, God is not a woman. Nobody knows what God is.
That is the reason why in many scriptures, God is referred to as "it".
God did not make man in his own image. Instead, man made God in his own image.
To say that "God is a father" or "God is a mother" is strictly to help a devotee concentrate on God during the initial stages of his or her devotion.
God is subtle, eternal, infinite, unnameable, and omnipresent.

In the Rig Veda, it is written:
"God is One, whom the learned call by various names."
Meaning,
One God expresses itself in trillions of forms
with trillions of names.

The Svetasvatara Upanishad 4:20 reads: "His form is not to be seen; no one sees Him with the eye." The Yajur Veda 32:3 reads: "There is no image of Him." When a devotee progresses in his/her devotion, the devotee will see that the God he or she is seeking has nothing to do with human attributes.

If what you say is true, why do they say Hindus are actually worshipping idols?

I cannot blame them for their misunderstanding. Once upon a time, Jewish society was plagued by Jews literally worshipping idols of Egyptian gods such as Baal and El, Canaanite gods, as well as other Roman and Babylonian gods. So Jehovah—or God, whom Moses met on the mountain top—asked Moses to kill anyone who was worshipping any god other than Jehovah.

The Jews always worshipped many gods, even after their departure from Egypt, and the Old Testament states that Moses killed everyone who worshipped any God other than Jehovah (Numbers 31).

So, if anyone bows in front of any idol, they are breaking the laws of the Old Testament (Leviticus 26:1 and Exodus 20:2–5.) This is the reason why people belonging to Abrahamic religions look down on any worship using idols: they're comparing what happened in their own religion's history to what is happening in India. In India, we do not worship idols as gods. We use idols strictly to concentrate on a God who has no name or form.

> Lord Krishna said:
> "That yogi who worships me with the understanding that I am situated in all beings as Atman remains always in me in all circumstances."
> (6:31)

> Lord Krishna also said to Arjuna:
> "Unable to comprehend my imperishable state as the Brahman, the unmanifest, ignorant people regard me as having manifested as Krishna. Ignorant people do not know that I am unborn and infallible."
> (7:24–25)

Arjuna very specifically asks Lord Krishna whether one should worship God as a person or worship God as impersonal.

Arjuna asked:
"O Krishna, who has the best understanding of salvation:
those who worship you as Lord Krishna or those who
worship you as the impersonal, formless, imperishable
Brahman?"
(12:1)

Rishis knew that ordinary people with simple, untrained minds would find it difficult to concentrate on a nameless and formless God. Thus the rishis allowed the use of idols during worship as a point of concentration so that these people could focus their minds, meditate, and communicate with God. The rishis also knew that when people progressed in their devotion, their personal God would transform to a nameless and formless God and that eventually, the devotee would merge with God. This has happened in the lives of all mystics, including Sage Valmiki, Ramakrishna Paramahamsa, Chaitanya, and even in the life of Sage Narada. And that is exactly what Lord Krishna said to Arjuna:

Lord Krishna answered:
"Those who worship me with great faith, I consider them
to be perfect. However, those who worship the impersonal,
formless, imperishable Brahman with proper control of
their senses also will finally attain me.
Arjuna, remember that those whose minds are attached
to the impersonal, formless, imperishable Brahman will
find it very difficult to progress in their path, since they are
born with a body and mind and as such visualizing God as
nameless and formless is difficult."
(12:2–5)

What happens when we pray?

That is an excellent question. Let me explain to you stage by stage what happens to someone who prays to God.

First Stage	People always start by praying to a very personal God.
Second Stage	As the devotee matures spiritually, the personal God will transform into light in the mind of the devotee.
Third Stage	The personal God will transform into nothing or a void in his or her mind.
Fourth Stage	Finally, the devotee will realize that he or she is one with God. At that time, the devotee will say *Aham Brahmasmi* (I am God.) All mystics, including Jesus Christ, have said "I am God."

Even Sage Narada felt "I am God," and this is the reason that he wrote: "God, I know you and I are essentially one, but still I like to keep away from you, so that I can enjoy the magnetic attraction between us."

At the end, everyone will realize "Aham Brahmasmi" meaning "I am God". This transformation will happen in the lives of everyone, irrespective of whether or not one is a Hindu.

Lord Krishna also said to Arjuna: "Unable to comprehend my imperishable state as the Brahman, the unmanifest, ignorant people regard me as having manifested as Krishna. Ignorant people do not know I am unborn and infallible."
(7:24–25)

Rishis knew that ordinary people with simple untrained minds would find it very difficult to concentrate on a nameless and formless God so rishis allowed the use of idols during worship.

Rishis also knew that when people progress in their devotion their personal God will transform to a nameless and formless God and eventually the devotee and God will become one.

Why do Hindus worship idols?

Hindus do not worship idols.

Like everybody else, Hindus use idols to worship the God who is nameless and formless.

God is not a man;
God is not a woman;
Nobody knows what God is.

God is subtle, eternal, infinite, unnameable, formless, and omnipresent.

All worship starts with idols and a personal God. But when a devotee progresses in his or her devotion the devotee will realize that the God he or she is seeking has nothing to do with any human attributes.

God said:

"Call me by whatever
name you like;
Worship me in any
form you like;
All that worship goes to
the One and
Only Supreme Reality."

Why do Hindus worship many gods?

Hindus do not worship many gods. Hindus worship one god, Brahman, with many names and in many forms.

Brahman can be neither described nor conceived by human faculties.

All of us are totally different, and as such, the rishis (ancient Hindu seers) allowed Hindus to worship God with whatever name and in whatever form they wanted.

Rig Veda (1:164:46) states:
"Ekam Sat, Viprah Bahudha Vadanti."
God or Truth is One, theologians call God by many names.

Chapter 35

What does Lord Krishna say about the food we eat?

Details	Verse
Yoga and a balanced diet	6:16
Diet and the gunas	17:7–10
Offerings and Brahman	4:24
Brahman and digestion	15:14

Grandson: Does Lord Krishna say anything about what food we should eat?

Grandfather: Amazing as it may sound, Lord Krishna discusses many details about food and what food we have to eat in the Bhagavad Gita. Ayurveda, the Hindu medicinal book, also deals with food in detail.

The Vedas, as well as Adi Sankara, consider the human body to be a gift from God, and it is the duty of everyone to take care of their bodies and minds. Even though people starve in large numbers throughout the world, many people who have food to eat have the habit of eating too much or eating the wrong food. Food has to be consumed moderately. Ayurveda recommends occasional fasting to everyone.

Lord Krishna discusses the importance of healthy living as follows:

Lord Krishna said:
"O Arjuna, Yoga is not possible for the ones who eat too much, or who do not eat at all; Yoga is not possible for the ones who sleep too much, or who keep always awake."
(6:16)

Lord Krishna divides food into three categories. According to him, foods which are too bitter, sour, salty, pungent, dry, and hot can lead to pain, distress, and disease of the body.

Lord Krishna said:
"Arjuna, there are three kinds of food that people prefer, according to their three gunas.
Foods that promote health, life, virtue, strength, happiness, and satisfaction are juicy, fatty, wholesome, and pleasing to the heart. These foods are dear to people who are sattvic in nature (people who are pure and spiritual).
Foods that are salty, hot, pungent, dry, excessively bitter, too sour, and burning are dear to those who are rajasic in nature (people who are excitable and passionate). Such foods cause pain, sorrow, distress, misery, and disease.
Foods that are stale, prepared more than three hours before being eaten, tasteless, decomposed, rotten, or left over by others are dear to people who are tamasic in nature (people who are lazy)."
(17:7–10)

Like everybody else, Hindus also offer food to God before eating it. Sri Satya Sai Baba highly recommends that every Hindu chant the following verses from the Bhagavad Gita before eating any food:

Lord Krishna said:
"The solemn act of offering is Brahman. The offering itself is Brahman. The offering is done by Brahman in the sacred fire which is Brahman. He alone attains Brahman who, in all actions, is fully absorbed in Brahman."
(4:24)

Lord Krishna said:
"I reside as the fire of digestion in the bodies of all living entities, and I join with the air of life, outgoing and incoming, to digest the four kinds of foods."
(15:14)

Hinduism does not glorify poverty

1.	Hinduism believes in charity (dana or giving) and treating guests as God (Athithi Devo).
2.	But Hinduism does not glorify poverty.
3.	Hinduism advocates austerity, simplicity, and detachment, but that has nothing to do with living in poverty.
4.	One of the four aims of life known as purusharthas is to earn and enjoy wealth (Artha).
5.	Hindu scriptures very clearly state human existence is not possible without wealth.
6.	If Hinduism glorifies poverty, King Janaka who was a very rich king would never have been treated as a great rishi in Hindu scriptures.
7.	If Hinduism glorifies poverty, people would not pray to Goddess Lakshmi for wealth.
8.	If Hinduism glorifies poverty, Hindu kingdoms would not have been dazzling in wealth.

Chapter 36

What happens to people who stray from their spiritual pursuits?

Details	Verse
Death and spiritual pursuit	6:37–42, 44–45

Grandson: According to Lord Krishna, what happens to someone who strays from his or her spiritual pursuit?

Grandfather: Lord Krishna discusses this question in detail. As far the Holy Bible is concerned, a Christian who strays will lose his or her right to salvation and go to hell for eternity, whereas Hindu scriptures state that salvation is the birthright of everyone, the best among us as well as the worst among us.

Arjuna asks: What happens to a person who dies at the end, deviating from spiritual pursuits and indulging in all kinds of material pleasures?

Arjuna asks:
"O Krishna, what about a man of faith who could not control his mind, who deviated from the spiritual path and failed to attain self-realization, and died. What will happen to him?
Do you think this man who has fallen away from both spiritual and material pursuits will perish like a riven cloud, with no solid footing in anywhere?

Dear Krishna, this is my doubt, and I ask you to dispel it completely. Nobody else can answer this question."
(6:37-39)

Lord Krishna answers that such a man will never perish. He will be reborn into a family of pure, pious people after living many years in heaven, and he will continue his spiritual quest where he left off in his last life.

Lord Krishna answered:
"Arjuna, he who strays from spiritual pursuits and dies will attain heaven. Later, he will be born into an aristrocratic family of high culture and spiritual values, where he will be able to continue the spiritual pursuits he left off in the last life. Under no condition is he lost. Once you step on the ladder of spirituality, you will only go forward, never backward."
(6:41-45)

Nobody is lost or goes to hell permanently in Hinduism. Even the worst among us will one day attain salvation.

According to Hindu scriptures, salvation is for all. Nobody, even those who have nothing to do with Hinduism, is denied salvation.

The best among us will attain salvation with one life, and the worst among us will attain salvation through many lives. The only difference between the best and the worst is the time factor.

Chapter 37

Did the father of the atom bomb really quote from and read the Bhagavad Gita?

Details	Verse
"Hundreds of thousands of suns."	11:12
"I am death, the mighty destroyer of the worlds."	11:32–33

Grandson: Is it a fact that Robert Oppenheimer quoted the Bhagavad Gita after witnessing the very first nuclear explosion?

Grandfather: Yes, he did. Robert Oppenheimer was the director of the Manhattan Project as well as the father of the atom bomb during the Second World War. He was a great admirer of the Bhagavad Gita, and studied it in original Sanskrit. He was taken by its charm and its general wisdom.

Oppenheimer really shocked the world when he quoted a couplet from the Gita (11:12) after witnessing the first atomic explosion at the Alamogordo bombing and gunnery range in New Mexico on July 16, 1945. Maybe it was a strange coincidence that the code name of the nuclear test was "Trinity", a name assigned by Oppenheimer. Was he thinking of Lord Vishnu and the Hindu Trinity? We will never know.

What Oppenheimer quoted on seeing the explosion was Sanjaya's description to the blind king, Dhritarashtra, of the form of God he saw in the battlefield:

> Sanjaya said:
> "If hundreds of thousands of suns were to rise at once into the sky, their radiance might resemble the splendor and radiance of the mighty Lord in that universal form."
> (11:12)

Later, when he addressed the US Congress regarding the atom bomb, he said it reminded him of Lord Krishna, who said in the Bhagavad Gita: "I am death, the mighty destroyer of the worlds." (11:32)

> Lord Krishna said:
> "I am death, the mighty destroyer of the worlds. I have come to destroy these people who are assembled to fight with you. Even without you taking part, all the soldiers of the Kauravas will be slain.
> Therefore, rise up and prepare to fight. Defeat your enemies and enjoy a flourishing kingdom. Please note that I have already killed everyone in the opposing army, Arjuna. You are just my instrument."
> (11:32–33)

Oppenheimer was raised as a Jew, and he never converted to Hinduism or had anything to do with Hinduism. Still, he was deeply affected by the Bhagavad Gita and by its teachings in his later life.

What is Namaste?

It is the popular Hindu greeting performed by pressing two hands together and holding them near the heart. The whole act communicates to the world:

"You and I are one. I salute and worship the God within you which is a mirror image of me."

Everything about Hinduism is reflected in "Namaste" since it proclaims to the world that the real "I" is the immortal soul (Atman) within the body and not the physical body.

Chapter 38

Why don't Hindus convert others to their religion?

Details	Verse
"Whatever path people take to worship me, I reward them accordingly."	4:11

Grandson: Why don't Hindus convert others to their religion? What did Lord Krishna say about that?

Grandfather: Excellent question. It is true that many religions resort to conversion, even sometimes doing so by force. But Hindus do not do that.

As I said, Hinduism is a culture or a "way of life" that includes many religious traditions within it. Islam and Christianity are organized religions with a founder, one major holy book each, and a very controlling hierarchy. Hinduism has no founder, no Pope, and no hierarchy. Hinduism just has a lot of scriptures.

"Absolute freedom of thoughts and actions" is the cardinal principle of Hinduism. Even an atheist has the right to condemn Hinduism in public and still proudly say that he or she is a Hindu.

Hindus rarely talk about their faith in public and always respect other religions and their holy scriptures. Of all the religions in the world, Hinduism is extremely liberal, tolerant, and elastic. Nobody is thrown out of Hinduism: once a Hindu, you are always a Hindu.

In the Bhagavad Gita, Lord Krishna never, ever says that one has to be a Hindu to attain salvation. Instead, he very clearly states that he will reward a person irrespective of whatever faith he chooses to follow.

> Lord Krishna said:
> "In whatever path people take to worship me, I reward them accordingly. Everyone should follow my (God's) path."
> (4:11)

> In the Rig Veda, it is written:
> "God is One, whom the learned call by various names."
> Meaning:
> One God expresses itself in trillions of forms
> with trillions of names.

Do you mean to say that Hindus do not convert others to Hinduism at all?

I did not mean that. I meant that Hindus do not actively convert anyone to Hinduism. At the same time, Hindus welcome with open arms anyone who wants to join Hinduism.

So you mean to say that they are converting to Hinduism out of their own free will?

Exactly true. Some convert to Hinduism outright, such as the American actress Julia Roberts, whereas many do not convert but follow some aspect of Hinduism in their daily lives, such as the Beatles, Robert Oppenheimer, Albert Einstein, Niels Bohr,

Nikola Tesla, among others. It is said, for example, that Nikola Tesla, the inventor of alternating current, developed his ideas about unlimited, free energy after meeting with the famous Hindu monk, Swami Vivekananda, who visited the United States in the 1890s.

On August 15, 2009, Lisa Miller published an article called "We Are All Hindus Now". According to that article, there are two groups of people in the world: Hindus, and people who think of the world in a way that's relevant to the Hindu scriptures.

When people

search for truth,

they automatically

end up in

Hinduism, since

Hinduism is man's

everlasting search

for truth.

What attracts people to Hinduism?

The concept of
utmost freedom of
thoughts and
actions.

Even atheists have the freedom to condemn
Hinduism in public and still proudly say they are
Hindus.

When Romans were feeding Christians to lions in Rome, Christians were worshipping in churches in Kerala, India.

According to a very ancient Syriac work *The Acts of Judas*, during 52 CE Apostle Thomas (Doubting Thomas) came to a place very close to Cochin, Kerala, India, and later established churches all over Kerala.

He travelled to China and finally died at Mylapore, Madras, in 72 CE.

Hindus do not convert anyone to Hinduism.

Those who convert are those who have fallen in love with Hindu concepts and Hindu beliefs, such as Julia Roberts.

Everyone is attracted to Hinduism since there are no restrictions whatsoever in it. Everyone has the right to believe whatever he or she wants to believe and worship God in whatever form or under whatever name he or she wants.

Chapter 39

Why did Lord Krishna say that "women are of lower birth"?

Grandson: Why did Lord Krishna say that "women are of lower birth"? Don't you think that's demeaning to women?

Grandfather: There are only two verses about women in the entire Bhagavad Gita. Before discussing what the Bhagavad Gita said about women, I have to stress the following points.

Women were always kept on a pedestal in India. The worship of the Mother Goddess Sakti started during the Rig Vedic Period, and apart from that, there were numerous women such as Gargi, Maitreyi, Ghosha, Lopamudra, and Indrani who displayed incredible intellect, skill, and devotion, far surpassing that of their male counterparts.

At the same time, throughout the world men have never fully understood women. For example, in all the scriptures, there is a lot of discussion about semen, but rarely do they discuss the female egg. It may be that nobody knew at that time that without a fertile female egg, conception and having a baby were totally impossible.

All laws restricting the freedom of women were written by men. For example, in Manu Smriti, Sage Manu wrote: "Women must always be honored and respected by the father, brother, husband, and brothers-in-law who desire their own welfare." But Manu also wrote: "A woman does not deserve liberty, since she is looked after by her father when she is a child, looked after by her husband after marriage, and looked after her by son when she is old."

Similarly, in Christianity, there were laws restricting the freedom of women, and women are treated very badly even today. St Paul in his first letter to the Corinthians wrote: "Women should remain silent in the churches. They are not allowed to speak, but must be in submission, as the law says." And he also wrote in the first letter to Timothy: "I do not permit a woman to teach or to assume authority over a man; she must be quiet." The Catholic religion has yet to permit its first woman priest.

Arjuna brought up the issue about women in the Bhagavad Gita, showing his concern about women going astray after a great war where many fighters will die. (1:41) Later, an eyebrow-raising verse describes women as being of "lower birth." (9:32)

> Lord Krishna said:
> "Arjuna, those who take shelter in me, though they are of lower birth such as women, Vaishyas, and Sudras, can attain salvation."
> (9:32)

Please remember that the Bhagavad Gita was written by Rishi Veda Vyasa, and like everybody else, he stated the prevailing beliefs at the time when this great scripture was written. During that period, Brahmins and Kshatriyas were treated with much more respect than women, Vaishyas, and Sudras. As far as I am concerned, those prevailing beliefs are what this statement reflects.

I do believe that men and women are very different in thinking as well as their actions. I may not go so far as to say "Men are from Mars and women are from Venus," but normally men have no clue to what women are thinking. This may have something to do with how a female brain and a male brain are wired.

Still, this particular verse should not be of concern to anybody.

After all, we are essentially immortal souls, even though we come to this world as man and woman. All of us have one common goal, which is to eradicate samsara and become one with God. Whether we are men or women, the only thing we have to be concerned with is to attain salvation.

All scriptures are written by men, and sadly, even those scriptures show the ignorance that men have about women's bodies and minds.

What is the original name of Hinduism?

Sanatana Dharma was the original name of Hinduism. It was the Persians who came to India during the sixth century BCE who began using the name "Hinduism" to refer to the religion of the people living near the Indus river.

In the Persian language, the letters *h* and *s* are pronounced almost the same, so they mistook the word Sindhu (the Sanskrit name for the Indus river) for Hindu.

There are no words Hindu or Hinduism in any of the Hindu scriptures.

The Christian "born again concept" is somewhat similar to the Hindu concept of Dwija (twice born) and the Hindu Upanayanam ceremony.

Upanayanam also represents a "spiritual rebirth" and henceforth it is called "Dwija" or "twice born" ritual.

Upa means "next" and Nayanam means "eye", hence the Upanayanam symbolizes the opening of the third eye or the eye of knowledge in the child.

Upanayanam is called literally "near-sight" and also called "sacred thread ceremony".

What the rishis and Jesus Christ taught is one and the same. "Unless there is a complete change of consciousness from material to spiritual, nobody can attain self-realization."

Chapter 40

Does the Bhagavad Gita mention the Vedas?

Details	Verse
The Vedas, self-realization, and ritualistic performance	2:42–3, 46
Karma and the Vedas	3:15
Vedas and salvation	4:32
I am also the Rig, the Sama, and the Yajur Vedas	9:17
"Among the Vedas, I am Sama Veda"	10:22

Grandson: Does the Bhagavad Gita mention the Vedas?

Grandfather: Yes: the Rig, Sama, and Yajur Vedas are mentioned in the Bhagavad Gita. The Brahma Sutra is also mentioned in verse 13:5, and Lord Krishna mentions Vedanta in verses 15:5 and 18:13.

There is no mention of the Atharva Veda throughout the 700 verses of the Bhagavad Gita. None of the Upanishads is mentioned either.

Why there is no mention of the Atharva Veda in the Bhagavad Gita?

Very good question indeed. It's possible that there was no Atharva Veda when the Gita was written, or the Atharva Veda might have been considered less important since it was written by Sage Atharvan alone. But whatever the reason, the Atharva Veda is generally less predominant than the other Vedas.

Lord Krishna looks at the Vedas as a tool to acquire knowledge, while at the same time, he looks down on people who are very boastful about their familiarity with the Vedas.

Lord Krishna said:
"O Arjuna, those who delight in the flowery words of the Vedas, follow the Vedas verbatim, and believe that there is nothing more than what is taught in Vedas...
They are full of desires and consider the attainment of heaven or attaining a good birth in the next life as the highest goal of life. Thus they are attached to ritualistic performances of the Vedas."
(2:42–43)

"To a self-realized person, the Vedas are not useful. What is the use of a small reservoir of water when a huge lake is available?"
(2:46)

Lord Krishna also said:
"Karma is prescribed in the Vedas. The Vedas came from God or Brahman. Thus the all-pervading Brahman is ever present in Yajna, or service."
(3:15)

"Many types of sacrifices and rituals are described in the Vedas. Know them all to be actions to be done by the body, mind, and senses. Knowing this, you shall attain salvation."
(4:32)

Lord Krishna also places more importance on the Sama Veda

than the other two Vedas.

> Lord Krishna said:
> "Among the Vedas, I am Sama Veda. Among Devas, I am Devandra. Among senses, I am the mind. Among the living beings, I am the consciousness."
> (10:22)

> Lord Krishna said:
> "I am the father of this universe, its mother, and the grandfather. I am knowledge (jnana) and the syllable Aum. I am also the Rig, the Sama, and the Yajur Vedas."
> (9:17)

The Rig Veda, Sama Veda, and Yajur Veda are mentioned in the Bhagavad Gita.
The Atharva Veda is not mentioned in the Bhagavad Gita.

Brahma Sutra is mentioned in verse 13:5.
In verses 15:5 and 18:13, Lord Krishna mentions Vedanta.
None of the Upanishads is mentioned by name in the Bhagavad Gita.

Among the six Hindu philosophies, it is Sankhya philosophy which is mentioned many times in the Bhagavad Gita.

In verse 10:26, Lord Krishna said:
"Among siddhas (perfected beings) I am Kapila, the founder of Sankhya philosophy."

Chapter 41

What are Raja Yoga and pranayama?

Details	Verse
Apana and prana	4:29
"This royal knowledge, this kingly secret"	9:2

Grandson: What is Raja Yoga?

Grandfather: Raja Yoga is one of the four yogas. Remember, Hindus have four yogas or paths to follow to attain salvation, defined as realizing the unity of the immortal soul and God. They are:

Jnana Yoga	Path of knowledge
Karma Yoga	Path of selfless actions
Raja Yoga	Path of breath control and pranayama
Bhakti Yoga	Path of devotion

Of all the four yogas, Lord Krishna gave the utmost importance to Raja Yoga, describing it as a royal secret.

> Lord Krishna said:
> "This royal knowledge, this kingly secret is the purest of all knowledge. It is directly perceivable,
> easy to practice, and imperishable."
> (9:2)

What is pranayama? Did Lord Krishna say anything about pranayama?

Pranayama comes from two separate Sanskrit words: prana, or "breath", and ayama, or "to stop". The rishis learned that breathing and thoughts are very closely connected, so they developed pranayama exercises to control breath and indirectly control thoughts as well as the mind.

Whenever we get angry, whenever we become emotional, whenever we become sad, we have to watch our breathing patterns. They will be erratic and rapid. When we immerse ourselves in spirituality, we will see that the breaths we take are deep and long. When we take deep breaths, we are less angry, less emotional, and more peaceful.

Raja Yoga teaches that our thoughts are deeply affected by our breathing patterns. When our breathing is fast and shallow and short, we will become very emotional, angry, and sad. The reverse is equally true.

> Lord Krishna said:
> "Some offer inhalation (Apana Vayu) into exhalation (Prana Vayu) and vice versa, resulting in the stoppage of all breathing. Others, curtailing the eating process, offer the outgoing breath into itself as a sacrifice."
> (4:29)

What is Yoga?

Sage Pathanjali wrote in Patanjali Yoga Sutra:

"Yoga Chitta Vrithi Norodha."

Yoga	means	union with the divine
Chitta Vrithi	means	mental vibrations
Nirodha	means	to stop

So yoga or self-realization means stoppage of mental activity, when a person sees everything as one (Advaita) and is not affected by dualities such as cold or hot, happiness or unhappiness.

What are the chakras?

According to the yogic and Tantric traditions of India, chakras are the whirling centers of energy located in the subtle body of every human being.

1.	Each chakra vibrates or rotates at a different speed.
2.	The root or the first chakra (with four petals) rotates at the slowest speed and the Crown Chakra (Sahasrara Chakra with 1000 petals) rotates at the fastest speed.
3.	Each chakra has its own color.
4.	There are seven chakras in the body and the seventh chakra (Sahasrara Chakra) is located slightly above the top of the head.

Chapter 42

What is the Hindu view on homosexuality?

Grandson: I am sorry, but I have to ask you a question about homosexuality. I hope you won't mind, but I am very curious. According to Christianity, it is a sin to be a homosexual. What are Lord Krishna's views on homosexuality?

Grandfather: You can ask me any question you have, and I will not judge you for the questions you ask. At your age, you should be asking millions of questions, and that is the only way to learn.

You also do not have to accept any answer anybody gives you. You have the right to investigate and come to your own personal conclusions. I am here only to answer questions on the basis of what is taught in our scriptures.

Before you start explaining the Hindu view on homosexuality to me, I would like to know how Hindus view human sexuality in general.

The Hindu aims of life are popularly known as purusharthas, or human goals. They are dharma (right conduct), artha (material gain), kama (sexual love), and moksha (salvation). Everyone tries to achieve all four goals in their life.

So sex is an integral part of life. As such, Hindus treat sex with the utmost respect, although sex became a taboo and any discussion of it became immoral after the Muslims and Christians came to India. But in contrast to other cultures, Hinduism does promote healthy sex between men and women.

What is the Kama Sutra?

The *Kama Sutra* is a book written by Sage Vatsyayana around the fourth century CE. It describes the daily routine of an ordinary man, complete with depictions of picnics, drinking parties, games, among others. The book also elaborately discusses the art of making love. Everything one can imagine about sex is described in this book. The author has gone to the extent of categorizing different forms of embraces, kisses, and types of women.

The intention of the author may be to teach a man how to woo a woman to become his bride, but many of his writings are against the fundamental ideas of Hinduism. Many Hindus do not even acknowledge this book as a part of Hinduism, since they fear it can lead to spiritual decline rather than help men in their married lives.

Thanks, Grandpa. Now, can you continue telling me about the Hindu view of homosexuality?

Lord Krishna did not deal with such subjects at all. It is indeed a very controversial subject to discuss, so you will not see many books about Hinduism discussing homosexuality.

Homosexuality is explicitly mentioned in only a few of the Hindu scriptures. Narada Smriti and Manu Smriti forbid homosexuality. Sage Manu wrote in Manu Smriti: "Dwijas (meaning Brahmins, Kshatriyas, and Vaishyas) should not engage in homosexuality."

Hindu scriptures discuss a third sex or third gender (tritiya-prakriti) literally, "third nature", or Napumsaka, meaning "neither male nor female". This category includes a wide range of people with mixed male and female natures such as effeminate males, masculine females, transgender people, the intersexed, and so on. The most well-known third gender group in India is called the Hijra, who live in north India.

In the Mahabharata, Arjuna was cursed to become a transgender woman called Brihannala for a year. Another hero in the Mahabharata was Shikhandi, who was born female but raised as a man. Because Bhishma said he would never fight any woman or transgender people, he refused to fight Shikhandi and died when hundreds of arrows were showered in him.

Why did Abrahamic religions condemn homosexuality?

Homosexuality has existed throughout human history, all across the world. Greek emperors like Alexander the Great, as well as most of the Roman emperors, were homosexuals. The Abrahamic religions condemned it as punishable by death, even though Jesus never mentioned it. Rather, it was St Paul—who had been a fanatic Jew until he converted to Christianity—who wrote against homosexuality in the New Testament.

In the Old Testament, the Book of Leviticus prohibits "lying with mankind as with womankind" and the story of Sodom and Gomorrah has historically been interpreted as condemning homosexual acts. This may be the explanation: initially, there were only twelve tribes of Jews in the land of Canaan, and they were involved in constant wars with everyone. The Jews wanted every man to get married and make as many babies as possible in order to save their traditions and culture. As such, they could not afford to have men falling in love with men and women falling in love with women. They badly needed young men to fight wars with their enemies, so they came out with strong condemnations of homosexuality.

Jews could not afford some men of their small tribe of 144,000 people becoming homosexuals. So the Abrahamic condemnation of homosexuality has to do with the social necessity of having a lot of able-bodied men to fight wars for their own protection. Because the Jews could not afford some men becoming homosexuals, any law made against homosexuality has to do with the survival of their culture and beliefs rather than religion. Those laws have nothing to do with spirituality.

Homosexuality and Judaism

It became a problem during early days of Jewish society since Jews could not afford some men becoming homosexuals when they were at war with everybody else around them. Jews badly needed men to protect their society and with many boys dying during childhood due to all kinds of childhood diseases and malnutrition, Jews were forced to make laws against homosexuality.

Jesus did not speak for or against homosexuality.

It was St Paul who was a fanatic Jew before he converted to Christianity. He condemned homosexuality.

India's Supreme Court should be congratulated for recognizing transgender people as a third gender in a landmark ruling in August 2015.

The Supreme Court further ordered the government of India to provide transgender people with quotas in jobs and education in line with other minorities, as well as key amenities.

A victory for transgender people is a victory for the whole of India.

Chapter 43

Is Sati, or Suttee, part of Hinduism?

Grandson: What is Sati?

Grandfather: Sati (or Suttee) is the most horrendous act of widows killing themselves by jumping—either by their own will or forced by others—into the funeral pyre of their dead husbands.

Believe it or not, Sati has nothing to do with Hinduism. To say Sati is a part of Hinduism is exactly like saying that the Salem witch trials and the Spanish killing of Mayans have something to do with the immortal teachings of Jesus Christ.

There is not even one scriptural statement concerning Sati in the Vedas, or the Upanishads, or the two epics, or in any of the eighteen Puranas.

If so, how did the name Sati originate?

The name Sati originated from the name of Sati, the youngest daughter of Daksha Prajapathi, who was born from the thumb of Lord Brahma. King Daksha had sixty daughters, and all of them, except Sati, married other Prajapathis, who were also the sons of Lord Brahma. Sati, against the wishes and command of her father, married Lord Shiva. That made King Daksha very angry, and he banished Sati from his palace.

King Daksha once conducted a very grand yajna (festival of prayer and sacrifice), to which all the relatives and dignitaries were invited, except for Sati and her husband Lord Shiva. Sati went to the Yajna uninvited, against the wishes of her husband

Lord Shiva. King Daksha did not even recognize her when she appeared at his palace gate. Sati felt insulted beyond her wildest imagination. Struck by profound sorrow and unable to take the humiliation, Sati killed herself by self-immolation.

This suicidal act of Sati or Dashayani (daughter of Daksha) has nothing to do with her husband Lord Shiva. But after that incident, the horrendous act of widows killing themselves by jumping into the funeral pyre of their dead husbands was called Sati or Suttee.

Are you sure the Hindu scriptures don't mention Sati?

If you go through every Hindu scripture, you will see that Sati is never mentioned.

Manu Smitri: Sage Manu was India's code-giver, and his book Manu Smriti has dealt with almost everything one can think of. There is no mention of Sati or Suttee anywhere in Manu Smriti.

Rig Veda: Some argue that the Rig Veda sanctions Sati based on verse 10:18:7. This verse is part of the funeral services in Hinduism. However, the text only states that the widow should sleep next to the body of the dead husband as an act of last *saha sayanam* (sleeping together). The texts continuing from this text never mention any act of Sati, and after the funeral, the widow is allowed to marry anyone she pleases.

Ramayana: In the Ramayana, after Lord Rama's father King Dasaratha dies, none of his three wives practice Sati. When the monkey-king Bali dies, his wife Tara does not commit Sati, but instead marries his brother Sugriva. When the demon King Ravana is killed, his wife Mandodhari does not kill herself.

Mahabharata: There is not even one true act of Sati in the whole epic poem of the Mahabharata where thousands of men got killed. Even though one hundred Kaurava princes, including Duryodhana, are killed, not even one Kaurava princess commits Sati.

The acts of wives of Lord Krishna committing suicide after the demise of Lord Krishna have nothing to do with Sati. All those wives of Lord Krishna were apsaras, celestial beings who were born on earth to help Lord Krishna kill all demons. Once Krishna left, there were no need for them stay on earth. That is the reason they killed themselves after Lord Krishna returned to Vaikunda, the abode of Lord Vishnu.

It is true that Queen Madri, the wife of King Pandu, jumps into the funeral pyre of her fallen husband and kills herself. But her suicide has nothing to do with Sati. She felt that she was responsible for the death of her husband who had been cursed by a dying saint to die if he ever had intercourse. What happened to King Pandu was not Madri's fault, but Madri killed herself out of remorse. King Pandu had another wife, Kunti, who did not kill herself, which clearly shows that Madri's suicide has nothing to do with Sati.

Savitri, the legendary heroine of Hinduism: When Savitri's husband Satyavan died, the God of Death, Yama, came to take the soul of Satyavan. Savitri engaged Lord Yama in a debate, and Yama was forced to let go of Satyavan. During this episode, there was absolutely no mention of Savitri committing Sati. That thought never occurred in her mind.

Then where did Sati come from?

Sati had its roots in Greece. Pyre services similar to Sati were also prevalent among Germans, Slavs, and other races. The practice of Sati came to India through the Kushans around 1 CE.

Who practiced Sati in India?

The Rajputs, a warrior tribe who were descendants of the Kushans and who were very fanatical, monogamous Hindus, were the ones who practiced Sati. Sati was never, ever practiced in south India.

222 • ED VISWANATHAN

Why did they practice Sati?

The Rajputs were in constant wars amongst themselves and with the Muslims. Because of that, there were thousands of young widows, and they feared that it would be dangerous to have thousands of young, beautiful widows running around. So they went to the extreme measure of eliminating them.

What happened to Sati?

In 1829, the British government in India, with the support of Raja Ram Mohan Roy, the Hindu reformer, outlawed Sati as a criminal offence. Copycats appear now and then, but believe me, the vast majority of people have nothing to do with Sati. If Sati was part of Hinduism, thousands of widows would have been killed all over India. That never, happened; there is no history to say otherwise.

Chapter 44

What does it mean to surrender to God?

Details	Verse
Surrender and freedom from desire	3:30
Surrender and reward	4:11
Surrender and sin	5:10
Surrender and maya	7:14
Surrender, dharma, and karma	18:66
Arjuna as an instrument	11:33

Grandson: What does it mean to surrender to God?

Grandfather: When we say "surrendering to God," some may feel we should act either irrational or become lazy. That is not true. Surrender is the quantum leap from mind to mindlessness, from ego to a state of no ego. To surrender ourselves to God means to allow God to work through us, or to do things according to our inner voice. Surrendering to God means to become an instrument of God.

How can one achieve that?

Lord Krishna describes in detail in many verses how to achieve that in the Bhagavad Gita.

Lord Krishna said:
"Arjuna, fight, surrendering all actions unto me, with full knowledge of the indwelling Atman (immortal soul) and free from desire, selfishness, and grief."
(3:30)

Lord Krishna said:
"Arjuna, in whatever way people surrender unto me, I reward them accordingly. Please know that everyone follows my path in all circumstances."
(4:11)

Lord Krishna said:
"One who works without any attachment and desire, surrendering the results of all actions unto me, is not tainted by sin, just as the lotus leaf is untouched by water."
(5:10)

Lord Krishna said:
"My maya, consisting of three gunas, is difficult to overcome. But those who have surrendered themselves to me (God) can easily surpass my illusion.
Those scoundrels who are grossly foolish, the lowest of men, who live under an illusion and who are atheists, do not surrender unto me."
(7:14–15)

Lord Krishna said:
"Abandon all dharma (duties) and just surrender unto me (the will of God). I shall deliver you from all bonds of karma. Do not fear."
(18:66)

Surrendering to God does not mean to run away from life. As the verse clearly states, it only means to perform all of our thoughts and our actions by taking refuge in God, making God the "doer" and you and I just servants of God. This is why spiritually mature people are very humble: all of their thoughts, words, actions, feelings, and everything are dedicated towards God.

By surrendering to God, we will automatically arrive at the answers to our questions regarding what to do and what not to do. If, when we eat our food, we first offer it to God, we will automatically stop eating food that is not appropriate. If we offer all of our actions to God, we will not take part in any illegal or unethical actions.

In the eleventh chapter of the Bhagavad Gita, Arjuna is baffled to see the whole Kaurava army dying in the mouth of the Viswaroopa, and he starts doubting why he has to fight the war.

Reading Arjuna's thoughts, Lord Krishna said to Arjuna:
"O Arjuna, be an instrument of God."
(11:33)

In other words, to eradicate the ego, we have no choice but to surrender ourselves to God and become an instrument of God.

Arjuna's problem was his ego.

He never surrendered himself to God and always thought he was doing everything.

Our problem is also our ego. The ego is the biggest stumbling block in our lives. Only by surrendering ourselves to God can we get rid of our ego.

Lord Krishna said:
"Arjuna, for one who sees me
(God) everywhere and sees
everything in me (God), I am
not lost to him,
nor he is lost to me (God)."
(6:30)

The demon King Hiranyakasipu asked his son
Prahlad:
"Where is your God?"
Prahlad answered:
"Whenever you look, there is my God."

When Sufis (Muslim mystics) visited Mecca,
Muslim fakirs asked them to pray to God facing
east.
The Sufis answered:
"Whenever we look, we see the face of God."

Lord Krishna said:

**"My devotees ultimately
will attain me."
(7:23)**

What did Lord Krishna mean by those
words?

Anyone who sincerely searches for God will
finally merge with God.
At that time the devotee and God will become
one and the devotee will say
Aham Brahmasmi (I am God).

Arjuna, be an instrument of God.
(Nimitha-mattram bhava Savyasachin)

Lord Krishna said:
"Arjuna, just be an
instrument."
(11.33)

Only by surrendering ourselves to God and becoming an instrument of God can we deal with our problems in life. The more we allow our egos to take over our life, the more we suffer.

Chapter 45

What did Lord Krishna say about the five senses?

Details	Verse
The senses, attachment, and delusion	2:58–63
The senses as stumbling blocks	3:34
Offering the senses to mental control and Yoga	4:26–27

Grandson: What did Lord Krishna say about the five senses?

Grandfather: The five senses—smell, taste, touch, sound, and sight—are indeed the gifts of nature. Those senses can make us or destroy us. The only way we can mature spiritually is to control them.

There are no taboos about sex in Hinduism as there are in other religions, and Hinduism deals with sex in an extremely detailed manner through books like the *Kama Sutra*. Still, the Bhagavad Gita deals at length with the negative power of the senses and how to deal with them.

Lord Krishna said:
"When one can completely withdraw the senses (indriyas) from sense objects, as a tortoise withdraws its limbs into the shell for protection, then the intellect of such a person is considered steady."
(2.58)

Sadly, most people live a life which is totally controlled by the sense organs, which leads to feelings of love (ragas) and hate (dwesha) towards different objects. The senses are constantly being motivated by the force of attraction and aversion.

Lord Krishna said:
"Arjuna, suppression of desires is dangerous. Sublimation of desires is the best way. The desire for sensual pleasures fades away if one abstains from sense enjoyment, but the craving for sense enjoyment remains. The craving also disappears from one who surrenders himself or herself to God.
Arjuna, the restless senses (indriyas) are extremely clever and they can dupe even a very discriminating person. As such, one should fix one's mind on God after bringing the senses under control."
(2:59–61)

Lord Krishna narrates how a person slowly degenerates under the power of the senses. He warns that attachment to objects will only make our lives miserable.

Lord Krishna said:
"When one thinks about a sense object, attachment to that object is born. From attachment, desire is born, from desire comes frustration, and from frustration comes delusion. When one is deluded, one loses memory, and when one loses memory, the power of discrimination is lost. With the destruction of the power of discrimination, one falls from the righteous path."
(2:62–63)

Lord Krishna also tells Arjuna that only a person who has his or her senses under control will at that stage have all sorrows destroyed. (2:64–65)

> Lord Krishna said:
> "Each sense organ (indriya) has a love and hate relationship with objects. One should not live under such attachment and aversion of objects because they are the stumbling blocks on the path of spiritual maturity and self-realization."
> (3:34)

> Lord Krishna said:
> "Some yogis offer the senses of hearing into the fire of mental control.
> Others offer the functions of all sense organs in the fire of self-restrained yoga, which is ignited by jnana (knowledge)."
> (4:26–27)

Lord Krishna is not asking us to live like hermits. He is advising us to have a balanced life with everything done in a balanced manner. Yoga is not for those who are sleeping all the time or not sleeping at all. Yoga is not for those who are not eating at all or eating all the time.

Eating like a glutton, neglecting one's studies, constantly staying on social media like Facebook, texting, drinking, and using drugs are all examples of a life controlled by sense organs. To live a life totally controlled by the senses is the worst thing one can do. But a person who embarks upon the path of spiritual maturity and self-realization should never fall under the influence of the dualities of the senses.

Chapter 46

When is the best time to study, pray, and meditate?

Grandson: Grandpa, when is the best time to study, pray, and meditate? Your answer can really help me in my studies.

Grandfather: It is written that we get maximum benefits when we do things during Brahma Muhurta, the time between 3 a.m. and dawn. In fact, I wrote my entire book *Am I a Hindu?* during Brahma Muhurta.

There are varied opinions about exactly which hours constitute Brahma Muhurta. Some say Brahma Muhurta is a period of two Muhurtas (time unit of forty-eight minutes), or about one and a half hours before dawn. Some say Brahma Muhurta starts at 3 a.m. and ends at 6 a.m. The tradition associated with Sivananda Yoga says it begins at 4 a.m. The tradition of Surat Shabda Yoga includes 3 a.m. through dawn in the amrita vela ("elixir" or "ambrosial" hours, as Brahma Muhurta is also known.) As this is the tradition into which I have been initiated, this is the time span I will consider in this exploration.

In the Brahmanas (the collection of ancient Indian texts with commentaries on the four Vedas), it is written that the Muhurta measurement denotes one-thirtieth of a day, or a period of forty-eight minutes. Brahma Muhurta is said to be the time when celestial beings rest and there is less "thought activity" in the ether. As such, we can think clearly and meditate very well.

As I have said, we are all a combination of the three gunas: sattva, rajas, and tamas. Brahma Muhurta is the time when sattva manifests itself in us and comes to the forefront. It is the ideal time for thinking and reflection on the truths laid down in Vedanta. Rajas manifests itself after 6 a.m., when the day's activities begin, children have to get ready for school, mothers have to prepare food for the family, and officegoers begin getting ready for work. These mark the beginning of a cycle of frenetic activity. It is after sundown that tamas begins to manifest itself.

Does Lord Krishna say anything about Brahma Muhurta?

No, he does not. However, as I explained, he says that the best time for death is during the six months when the sun travels north, and the worst time is during the six months when the sun travels south.

Atman and koshas

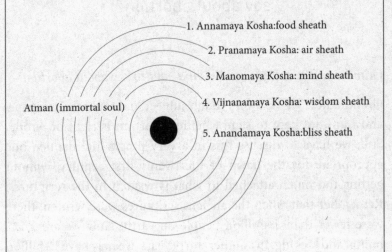

Atman (immortal soul)

1. Annamaya Kosha: food sheath
2. Pranamaya Kosha: air sheath
3. Manomaya Kosha: mind sheath
4. Vijnanamaya Kosha: wisdom sheath
5. Anandamaya Kosha: bliss sheath

Long before the birth of any medical science, our rishis knew that our human body consists of five layers called koshas that range from the dense physical body to the more subtle levels of emotions, mind, and spirit.

These five sheaths are independent of the immortal soul within the body.

Chapter 47

What do the Hindu scriptures
say about abortion?

Grandson: What does Lord Krishna have to say about abortion?

Grandfather: This is a very tough subject to discuss for everyone, and I am not here to state whether abortion is right or wrong. Still, we have to discuss this in a very pragmatic manner, one appropriate for the dawn of the twenty-first century, without getting too much attached to what is written in the scriptures. Remember that when the ancient scriptures were written, there were fewer than 1 million people on earth. Now we are 7.125 billion and kicking. In another thirty years, we may have 12 billion people on earth. So let us face it: we have to have a pragmatic approach to the whole problem.

Since time immemorial, Hindus have considered children to be a gift from God. Villagers celebrated whenever a baby was born in the village, and the rishis told pregnant women, "You look radiant and beautiful since God blessed you with a child." Amazingly, in ancient India, no woman was asked: "Who is the father of the baby?" Every child was considered a gift from God, and just as is written in the Holy Bible, "Be fruitful and multiply," (Genesis 1:28) our saints only welcomed every birth.

The main goal of all of this was to populate the world with men—literally *men*. This was not meant as a putdown of women, but rather a recognition that there was an extreme shortage of men in the world: a large number of men died in battles, and more male babies than female babies died at birth or from infant diseases. Kings conducted the Putra Kameshti Yaga ceremonies for the birth of male offspring.

Hindus, like Buddhists and Jains, believe that all life is sacred, to be loved, revered and protected because all creatures are manifestations of the one and only God. Thus the Hindu scriptures condemn abortion, except when the life of the mother is in danger.

There are many prayers in the Rig Veda to guard the embryo. The Kaushitaki Upanishad considers abortion to be parallel to killing one's parents. The Atharva Veda states that the slayer of the foetus is among the greatest of sinners. In Manu Smriti, Sage Manu forbids abortion.

The Pancha Maha Patakas (five worst acts) described by the Hindu Puranas are:

1	Brahma Hathya	Killing a Brahmin
2	Sisu Hathya	Destroying an unborn foetus
3	Sura Pana	Drinking liquor
4	Swarna Steya	Stealing gold
5	Guru Talpa Gamana	Having sex with the guru's wife

In the Mahabharata, Ashwatthaman, the great son of Drona, guru of both the Pandavas and Kauravas, was cursed by Lord Krishna to live like an animal for millions of years when he tried to destroy the foetus of Abhimanyu's wife (the child later became King Parikshit, the last of the Pandava clan).

The Rig Veda states: "That embryo then becomes a part of the woman's self, like any part of her body; it does not hurt her; she protects and develops the embryo within herself. As she protects the embryo, so also is she protected. In Satapatha Brahmana, it is written, "The person who extracts an embryo is called an evildoer."

Yet even though the Hindu scriptures argue in favor of protecting the embryo by all means, the Ayurvedic book *Sushruta Samhita* recommends abortion in certain cases: when the embryo is known to be defective, and/or when there is no chance for a normal birth.

It is outright murder if someone uses abortion as an easy way of family planning.

The embryo becomes a foetus during the eighth week of pregnancy.

To abort or not to abort is not an easy decision, and only the mother—after listening to everyone's advice, including her doctor's—can make the final decision. The government or even her husband should not have any say in it. Her decision is final and everybody should respect it: no one on earth can question it.

"Love Thy Enemy."
The most powerful, thought-provoking words
from the Holy Bible.

Those words are the basis of the **law of karma**. Powerful thoughts of love will come back to you like a boomerang and make you a fortress of love.

So too with hate.

Powerful thoughts of hate will come back to you like a boomerang and make you a fortress of hate.

Gautama Buddha said:

"Hatred is not conquered by hatred at any time, but hatred is won by love; this is an eternal truth."

Chapter 48

Why does Lord Krishna tell Arjuna to become a yogi?

Details	Verse
Yoga and sensual pleasures	2:70
Yoga and asceticism	6:46

Grandson: Why does Lord Krishna tell Arjuna to become a yogi?

A yogi lives like a lotus leaf. Raindrops fall on a lotus leaf, but the leaf is not affected by the rain drops. Similarly, a yogi lives in the world, but the yogi is unaffected by the world. This is why Lord Krishna said: "Arjuna, become a yogi!"

Lord Krishna said:
"Just as the ocean is unaffected by the waters of innumerable rivers flowing into it, a yogi is unaffected by the sensual pleasures due to the positive and negative reactions to actions he or she does."
(2:70)

Lord Krishna said:
"A yogi is superior to an ascetic, greater than a jnani (person who follows Jnana Yoga), and superior to a person who is ritualistic. Therefore, O Arjuna, in all circumstances try to become a yogi."
(6:46)

Things come and go in a yogi's life, just as they do in everyone else's life. But a yogi does not exhibit any emotion when things are good or when things are bad. Many have no idea that they do not have to be a Hindu to become a yogi. If they fit the definition of a yogi, even billionaires and pretty models can be called yogis.

Lord Krishna said:

"Just as the ocean is unaffected by the waters of innumerable rivers flowing into it; similarly, a yogi is unaffected by the sensual pleasures due to the positive and negative reactions to actions he or she does."
(2:70)

A yogi lives like a lotus leaf. Raindrops fall on a lotus leaf but the lotus leaf is not affected by raindrops.
Similarly, a yogi lives in the world, but the yogi is unaffected by the world.

Lord Krishna said:

"Just like a lamp in a windless place does not flicker, a yogi who has subdued his mind remains steady in his meditation on Brahman."
(6:19)

A yogi's mind is always steady and balanced.

Rishi Vasistha told Lord Rama
in the Yoga Vasistha:

"Chit Chalathi Samsare;
Nichale Moksha Muchayathe."

"When chit (mind) vibrates;
This whole world comes to
existence;
When the mind stops
vibrating;
This whole world is
destroyed;
And the person attains
salvation.

Chapter 49

Does Lord Krishna mention heaven and hell in the Bhagavad Gita?

Details	Verse
War and the door to heaven	2:32, 37
Description of heaven	9:20–21
The gates that lead to hell	16:21:22

Grandson: Did Lord Krishna mention heaven and hell in the Bhagavad Gita?

Grandfather: Concepts of heaven and hell are the most complicated aspects of all religions and also of Hinduism. Even though the Upanishads and the six Hindu philosophies mention very little about them, heaven (swarga) and hell (naraka) are mentioned in all eighteen of the Puranas.

For Hindus, heaven and hell are temporary abodes where the soul resides for a very short period and comes back to earth again to take another body to exhaust all karmic debt. In contrast, for Christians, who do not believe in reincarnation, heaven and hell are permanent resting places after death: those who accept Jesus Christ as their savior will go to heaven and those who do not accept Jesus Christ will go to hell permanently.

To a Hindu, heaven and hell are not important at all since a Hindu knows at the end everyone, including the worst among us, will finally attain salvation.

Lord Krishna said:
"Arjuna, only fortunate warriors get the opportunity to fight a war like this, since this war can open the door to heaven."
(2:32)

Lord Krishna said:
"Arjuna, you have two choices. Either you will die in this battle with the Kauravas and will go to heaven, or having won the battle, you will enjoy victory on earth. Therefore, please stand up and fight."
(2:37)

Lord Krishna said:
"Those who are well versed in the Vedas and drink the Soma juice: seeking heavenly planets, they worship me indirectly. Totally purified of their sinful nature, they stay on the pious heavenly planet of Indra, where they enjoy godly delights."
(9:20)

Lord Krishna said:
"The three gates that lead you to hell are lust, anger, and greed. Therefore, one should abandon these three gates. A person who has escaped from these three gates performs actions conducive to self-realization and thereby attains the highest goal."
(16:21–22)

Now the question is: if the immortal soul (Atman) is eternal and cannot experience anything, how will it learn a lesson either in heaven or in hell? Therefore, I personally feel that heaven and hell must still be on earth, unless in heaven and hell the immortal soul is accompanied by some kind of a body that can experience pleasure and pain.

But according to the Hindu Puranas, there are fourteen worlds in the universe: the seven upper and the seven lower. The seven upper worlds are Bhuh, Bhavah, Swah, Mahah, Janah, Tapah, and Satyam; and the seven nether worlds are Atala, Vitala, Sutala, Rasatala, Talatala, Mahatala, and Patala.

Thus according to Hinduism, hell is not just one place but consists of several realms. The Bhagavata Purana describes them all as being beneath the earth. People who have committed bad deeds and accumulated negative karma are sent to hell to purify their souls. Hell is ruled by Yama, the Hindu God of Death.

In contrast to hell, heaven consists of several realms that have no suffering. The kingdom of heaven is ruled by the god Indra, and the soul experiences pleasure at every moment and is surrounded by beautiful celestial beings. As in hell, time spent in heaven is temporary. Once all of the surplus karma is exhausted, the soul leaves heaven to incarnate on earth.

It is not necessary that a human being reincarnates as a human being again. If a great karmic debt has accumulated, a person can be born as any lower life form, such as a tiger or a pig. As we have said, these cycles of birth, death, and reincarnation will continue until a person realizes he or she is the immortal soul within the body. At that time, the person attains salvation, or self-realization.

Heaven and hell are not permanent.

As far as Hindu scriptures are concerned, heaven and hell are temporary abodes where the soul resides for a very short period and comes back to earth again to take another body in order to exhaust all karmic debt and attain salvation.

For all others who do not believe in the immortality of the soul as well as in rebirth, **heaven** and **hell** are permanent resting places after death.

Chapter 50

What did Lord Krishna say about devotion to God?

Details	Verse
Worship by always focusing on God	6:47, 12:2, 12:7
Attributes of God	9:19
All worship is worship of God	9:22–23
Whatever you do, do as an offering	9:26–27
"My devotee will never perish"	9:31
To become absorbed in God	9:34
God as the source of everything	10:8

Grandson: What did Lord Krishna say about devotion to God?

Grandfather: First of all, Lord Krishna informed Arjuna that he is indeed God, Brahman, even though he appears as a very playful romantic figure. God appears to us in whatever form we worship that God. When someone worships God as Lord Krishna, God appears as Lord Krishna. When someone worships God as Jesus Christ, God appears as Jesus Christ. When someone worships God as Goddess Kali, God appears as Kali.

But beyond appearances, God is nameless and formless. God is not a man. God is not a woman. Nobody knows what God is.

Adi Sankara wrote that there is nothing but God. In *Vivekachudamani*, Adi Sankara wrote that Brahman or God alone is truth, that the world is unreal, and that ultimately there is no difference between Brahman and the individual self. Like Hindus, the Kabbalists, who follow an esoteric school of thought that originated in Judaism, also assert that God is not separate from us at all.

God is the inner reality, the immortal soul. When you search after God, you are actually searching within yourself.

The demon King Hiranyakasipu asked his son Prahlad: "Where is your God?" Prahlad answered: "Wherever you look, there is my God."

> Lord Krishna said:
> "Among all yogis, the one who devoutly worships me with his or her mind and intellect focused on me (God) and thinks of me is the most intimately united with me and considered to be the best devotee."
> (6:47)

Whatever we do when surrendering to God is devotion to God. God does not want your money, and God does not care how knowledgeable you are about the Vedas or Upanishads. Going to a temple is not mandatory unless it makes you happy. One need not even chant any mantras: a simple, sincere prayer is enough.

> Lord Krishna said:
> "Arjuna, I give heat, and I withhold and send forth rain. I am immortality. I am also death. I am that which you see and that which you do not see. I am both that which exists and that which does not exist."
> (9:19)

Lord Krishna said:
"Arjuna, but those who always worship me in a steadfast manner, who are always united with me in devotion, I take care of what they lack and preserve what they have. Those who worship other gods with faith are actually worshipping me (the true God), although they are doing their worship in an improper manner."
(9:22–23)

Lord Krishna said:
"If anyone offers me (the Brahman) with love, sincerity, and devotion a leaf, a flower, a fruit, or water, I will accept that offering.
Arjuna, whatever you do, whatever you eat, whatever you offer, whatever rituals you perform, do that as an offering to me."
(9:26–27)

Lord Krishna said:
"O Arjuna, my devotee will never perish."
(9:31)

Anyone who surrenders everything to God, irrespective of what religion he or she belongs to, has nothing to worry about.

Lord Krishna said:
"Arjuna, fix your mind on me (Brahman). Become my devotee. Offer your homage to me and worship me. Being completely absorbed in me, finally you shall come to me."
(9:34)

> Lord Krishna said:
> "I am the source of everything, both spiritual as well as material. Everything emanates from me. Realizing this, the wise always worship me."
> (10:8)

> Lord Krishna said:
> "Those who always fix their minds on me and always worship me are considered most perfect by me."
> (12:2)

> Lord Krishna said:
> "Those who worship me by dedicating all their activities unto me, having their minds fixed upon me, are delivered by me from the cycles of repeated births and deaths."
> (12:7)

In all forms of worship, ultimately the worshipper will transcend the name and form of his or her personal God. Look at the writings of St Francis of Assisi, or the Sufi mystics, or Lord Chaitanya, or Sri Ramakrishna Paramahamsa. Chaitanya Mahaprabhu prayed to Lord Krishna and Ramakrishna prayed to Mother Kali. But if one studies every devotional scripture, one can see that the Absolute they were after has no name and no form and is beyond human description. All of these worshippers started with their attachment to a personal God and finally ended up with a God that is timeless and formless.

Lord Krishna said:

"O Arjuna,

My devotee will never

perish. He is never lost."

(9:31)

Anyone who surrenders everything to God, irrespective of what religion he or she belongs to, has nothing to worry about at all.

What happens when we pray?

First stage: All devotees start by praying to a personal God with a name and form.

Second stage: As the devotee matures spiritually, that personal God will transform to light in the mind of the devotee.

Third stage: During the third stage of devotion, that light will transform to nothing or void in the devotee's mind.

Fourth stage: Finally, the devotee will realize he or she is one with God. At that time the devotee will say "Aham Brahmasmi" (I am God.) All mystics around the globe have said "I am God".

Lord Krishna said:
"Arjuna, whomsoever offers me a leaf, a flower, fruit or even water with love, devotion, and a pure heart, I accept that devotional offering." (9:26)

Lord Krishna was pleased by his childhood friend Sudama's (Kuchela) avil (beaten rice) with all kinds of insects and dirt in it. Lord Krishna even personally washed Sudama's dirty feet.

This shows that God is interested only in our sincere, whole-hearted devotion. God is not interested in our wealth or whether or not we go to any temple every day.

Athithi Devo Bhava.

(A Guest is God)

The most enchanting words of greeting guests from the *Taittiriya Upanishad* are:

Mathru devo bhava
(treat your mother as God),
pithru devo bhava,
(treat your father as God)
acharya devo bhava,
(treat your guru as God)
athithi devo bhava,
(treat your guest as God)

Chapter 51

Why are the Ashrama Dharmas important?

Grandson: What are Ashrama and the Ashrama Dharmas?

Grandfather: Ashrama and the Ashrama Dharma are the fundamental aspects of life.

According to the Hindu scriptures, human life is believed to comprise four stages based on physical and mental development. These are called the Ashramas, and every man must go through each of these stages—no exceptions!

> Lord Krishna said:
> "Arjuna, perform your prescribed duty (Ashrama Dharma),
> for doing so is better than inaction. One cannot even
> maintain one's body without any work."
> (3:8)

In fact, Hindu scriptures forbid people from skipping over any of the four stages, as laid out in the Manu Smriti.

Ashrama	Age	Duties
Brahmacharya	8 to 18	Student life. No sex. Time spent acquiring knowledge in scriptures and other academic learning.
Grahasthya	18 to 40	Married life. Taking care of wife and children. A person is supposed to take care of all his desires, such as artha (money) and kama (sexual desire) during this stage.

| Vanaprastha | 40 to 65 | After the completion of one's householder duties, one gradually withdraws from the world, freely shares wisdom with others, and prepares for the complete renunciation of the final stage. |
| Sanyasa | 65 to death | One completely withdraws from the world and starts dedicating oneself to spiritual pursuits, seeking self-realization and freedom from the cycles of birth and death. |

Sage Suka was dissuaded by his father, Sage Veda Vyasa, from jumping from Brahmacharya to Sanyasa without going through Grahasthya (married life) first, even though Sage Suka did not obey his father.

Even Adi Sankara was dissuaded by his mother for skipping over married life. When Adi Sankara was about to ascend to the Sarvatnya Peedam in Benares, Goddess Sarasvati made him answer all of the necessary questions regarding Grahasthya before ascending.

Chapter 52

How can we eliminate stress from our lives?

Grandson: How can we eliminate stress from our lives?

Grandfather: The very best way to manage stress is to practice breathing exercises every day.

From time immemorial, the rishis knew that breathing and thoughts are very closely connected. Whenever we get angry, whenever we become emotional, whenever we become sad, our breathing becomes erratic, short, and rapid. When we immerse ourselves in spirituality, we will take deep and long breaths, which will make us less angry and more peaceful.

How can I practice breathing?

The exercises are called Hamsa, which means "unpronounced". Thus this is a silent mantra: whether we are aware of it or not, we chant Hamsa all the time. *Ha* is the sound of the breath on our exhalations and *sa* is the sound of the inhalations.

Some reverse the Hamsa mantra and call it So'ham. In this mantra, we hear "hmmm" on the inhalation and a sighing "sa" on the exhalation. *Ham* means "I Am" and refers to the immortal soul within. When you breathe in with the sound *ham*, you bring the life force from outside into your inner world. You affirm your "I am-ness". *Sa* means "that" and refers to the outer world.

How can we practice Hamsa?

To begin practicing Hamsa, try to take deep breathing exercises whenever you can. During them, watch your inhalation and exhalation without interfering with the flow pattern of the air or nostril movements.

The results will be amazing. Initially, when you practice Hamsa, you may fall asleep. Later, however, you will start to experience thoughtless, peaceful moments. Finally, you will experience an unexplainable peace all the time. You will be totally surprised when this starts happening to you.

You can practice Hamsa any time you want and as much as you want. There are no restrictions whatsoever and no yamas or niyamas (dos and don'ts) attached to this exercise.

Why do Hindu women wear a dot on their foreheads?

That dot is supposed to be at the meeting point of the eyebrows. This is called **Ajna Chakra**, the sixth chakra, also known as the third eye.

Ajna comes from Sanskrit, meaning to know and command.

Everyone should protect the Ajna Chakra. Once upon a time, all men also used to protect that point with sandalwood paste. But later, women alone protected it.

When someone meditates on Ajna Chakra, the seat of "concealed wisdom", he or she will see the light.

That may be the reason why Jesus said (Matthew 6:22):

"...if therefore thine eye be single, thy whole body shall be full of light..."

Chapter 53

Does yoga lead to a balanced life?

Unlike other religions, which demand severe austerities on the part of aspirants, in Hinduism we take a balanced approach to day-to-day problems and spirituality. We never, ever ask people to run away from life or abandon life. Instead, the Hindu scriptures ask people to follow their svadharma and live a healthy life.

Yoga is only for those who have a balanced life.

> Lord Krishna said:
> "O Arjuna, yoga is not possible for the one who eats too much, or who does not eat at all; who sleeps too much, or who always keeps awake."
> (6:16)

> "You do not have to starve to become spiritual.
> You do not have to adopt severe austerities to become spiritual.
> You do not have to deny sex to your spouse to become spiritual.
> You do not have to wear saffron robes to become spiritual.
> You do not have to do anything extraordinary to become spiritual.
> Just live a very natural life, doing the svadharma you are destined to do."

Chapter 54

If I pursue a spiritual path, will I lose my friends?

Grandson: Grandfather, if I pursue a spiritual path, will I lose my friends?

Grandfather: True, initially you will lose a lot of friends. Many of your old friends may not be on the same wavelength as you. They will not be interested in the things you are interested in, and vice versa.

But the few friends that will come to you will be the cream of the crop, the ones you will enjoy chatting with and doing things together for ages. You will see a reflection of yourself in those new spiritual friends.

This happens in everybody's life. Instead of worrying about losing friends, people should celebrate their good fortune in being able to mature spiritually.

Remember, also, that the best friend you have is you yourself: meaning your inner self. This is the reason why Sri Aurobindo asked us to listen to our inner voice.

When you start maturing exponentially in your spiritual pursuits, you will see yourself suddenly surrounded with many new people. Those who come to you at that stage will not be friends but seekers. You will have become a magnet, and everyone will be attracted to you.

Spiritual laws are exactly like laws in physics or chemistry. Everything that is written in our scriptures regarding spirituality will happen in everybody's life. We cannot avoid that. Everything Lord Krishna taught us in the Bhagavad Gita is to help us mature spiritually only.

Bhagavad Gita and soma

Lord Krishna said:
"Those who are well versed in the three
Vedas (Rig, Sama, and Yajur), who drink the
Soma juice, and whose sins are cleansed,
worship me through sacrifices in order to
gain heaven. Reaching heaven, the abode
of Indra, they enjoy celestial heavenly
pleasures."
(9:20)

1.	Everything about soma is somewhat mysterious.
2.	Soma is a very ritualistic hallucinating drink, frequently mentioned in the Rig Veda in the chapter Soma Mandala with 114 hymns. The Rig Veda calls this fungal growth, the plant of the "God of gods."
3.	Soma juice is prepared by extracting juice from the stalks of a certain fungal growth of mushroom origin.
4.	A similar plant named Haoma is mentioned in the Zoroastrian scripture, Avesta.
5.	Soma juice is different from the regular alcoholic drink available in ancient India called Sura in Sanskrit.

Chapter 55

What can I say to someone who is depressed or suicidal?

Grandson: I am not talking about myself. I just want to know what to tell someone who is depressed or suicidal. All young people get depressed once in a while. Did Lord Krishna address subjects like depression and suicide?

Grandfather: I fully understand what you are saying. All of us have to know how to deal with depression as well as suicidal thoughts.

Every one of us will be depressed once in a while. To say one is not depressed at all is a lie. Even the prettiest girl may ask her mirror: "Mirror, mirror on the wall, who is the fairest of them all?" and get depressed for no reason at all.

Arjuna himself was depressed in the first chapter of the Bhagavad Gita, when he made a long speech to Lord Krishna full of arguments against fighting the war. Finally, overcome with pity for himself, he said: "I give up. My bow is falling from me. I am lost for words. I am depressed. I do not know what to do. Krishna, please help me."

Only then did Lord Krishna answer him. Lord Krishna did not interrupt Arjuna during his speech about why he should not fight the war. He only answered Arjuna when he said that he did not know how to handle the situation and needed Lord Krishna's help.

All of us should be like Lord Krishna. When a depressed person talks to us we should never interrupt that person. We should listen to everything they have to say, and then, when that person seeks help, give our advice. (And if the depression is too much to handle, we should urge that person to seek professional help.)

Once upon a time, depression was not a serious matter among Hindus. At that time, Hindu society was a feudal society similar to the one presented in the film *Koottukudumbam,* where all the members the family—including the grandfather, grandmother, uncles, aunts, brothers, sisters, and in-laws—all live together under one roof. At that time, everyone had so many people to discuss their problems with, people who could offer a shoulder to cry on, and an ear to listen to their problems. During that period, a boy did not marry a girl or vice versa. Instead of marrying each other, a boy and a girl would marry a family.

Those were bygone years. Today, everyone has to face the world all by himself or herself. Depression is a serious matter and people who are depressed sometimes will not even know they are depressed. It is normal to be depressed now and then due to the ups and downs of life. But if emptiness and despair have taken hold of your life and won't go away, then you have depression, and you have to seek professional help.

Some of the things Lord Krishna teaches us may help us to get rid of depression even before it takes root in us.

Lord Krishna said: "Arjuna, everything comes and goes in life. Happiness and unhappiness are temporary experiences that rise from sense perception. Heat and cold, pleasure and pain, will come and go. They never last forever. So do not get attached to them."

Lord Krishna said: "Attachment is bondage. Please do not get attached to anyone or anything. People will come and go in your life and even your best friend may one day find you boring. Nobody is perfect and you cannot blame them for the way they feel about you."

Lord Krishna also said: "Surrender yourself to God. Make God in charge of your life. In that way, you can eradicate or at least control your ego." In other words, you should do everything in a selfless manner. The minute you wait even for a thank you card, you are in deep trouble.

Understand all of us are different and each of us sees everything in a totally different manner. Your father, mother, sister, and others all see everything totally differently from you. So never complain.

Bad things happen to everyone. So do not compare your life with anyone's life. The grass isn't always greener on the other side of the bank and you will never know what others are going through in their lives. When I was working, I printed a board with the following statement: "Nothing is a must; Nobody is a must" and put it on my office wall for me to look at every day. What I meant was I am not that essential to my office or for my family, and neither is my office or my family essential to me. Past karmic debt made all of us come together and even led me to work in that office.

Avoid naysayers, critics, and gossip-mongers as much as you can, even if they are very close relatives. Exercising regularly, eating healthy, and taking time out for fun and relaxation will help to avoid depressive thoughts. An idle mind is indeed a devil's paradise, so please always keep yourself occupied with positive thoughts and do something all the time. Never allow yourself to have a dull, boring time during any day.

What about suicidal thoughts?

Suicidal thoughts are caused by extreme depression. One has to seek professional help long before someone reaches that state.

Hinduism does not approve of suicide. Manu wrote in Manu Smriti that offerings of water which are usually offered to the departed souls should not be offered to someone who commits suicide. But at the same time, spiritually motivated suicide was permitted in ancient India under certain conditions. Remember, that type of suicide is not at all motivated by envy or other selfish reasons.

Samadhi	Seeking death by entering a cave and entering into a kumbaka state (state of suspended breath).
Prayopravesa	Death by slow starvation.
Agnipravesa	Self-immolation. This is distinct from a Sati's suicide, which involved a pre-existing funeral pyre rather than a separate fire.

Arjuna said:

"O Krishna, since the mind is unsteady, turbulent, obstinate, and very strong, controlling the mind is more difficult than controlling the wind."
(6:34)

Lord Krishna answered:

"Arjuna, no doubt the mind is very difficult to control. However, it can be controlled by constant practice and detachment."
(6:35)

Chapter 56

Who is a guru, according to Lord Krishna?

Details	Verse
Gurus and jnana	4:34
Spiritual pursuit and gurus	17:14

Grandson: Who is a guru, according to Lord Krishna?

Grandfather: Lord Krishna did not say much about gurus, except in verses 4:34 and 17:14: where he asked people to respect gods, Brahmins, and masters.

Guru is a loosely used word in the world today. Bookish knowledge of scriptures alone does not make someone a guru, and many people who say they are gurus are merely teachers.

A true guru will behave like a Sthita Prajna (enlightened person), whom we discussed earlier and whom Lord Krishna described in the second chapter of the Bhagavad Gita. Anyone who does not fit that definition is not a guru but merely a teacher.

Lord Krishna said:
"Arjuna, acquire jnana (wisdom) through sincere devotion, through relentless questioning and service of the wise (teacher). Those who are realized masters will in turn impart you that jnana they have acquired."
(4:34)

> Lord Krishna said:
> "Arjuna, purity, cleanliness, simplicity, celibacy, non-violence, worship of God, and realized masters (gurus) are considered physical austerities a devotee should follow in his or her spiritual pursuit."
> (17:14)

In Hinduism, a guru actually means God incarnate, manifesting in a personal form to guide the aspirant. The word guru means "dispeller of darkness" in Sanskrit. The guru is seen as the one who "dispels the darkness of ignorance". Guru also means "he who illumines".

A very famous prayer reads: the guru is Brahma; the guru is Vishnu; the guru is Maheswara (the God of Annihilation); the guru is verily the Para-Brahman (Supreme God); salutations to that guru. The Gita states: "He who bestows that nature which transcends qualities is said to be a guru."

There is absolutely no need to search after a guru. When we mature spiritually, a guru will automatically come to us. Swami Vivekananda did not make Ramakrishna Paramahamsa his guru; instead, it was indeed Ramakrishna Paramahamsa who made Swami Vivekananda his disciple. Even the apostles did not seek Jesus Christ as a guru. Instead, it was Jesus Christ who made the fishermen into his apostles, telling them that he would make them "fishers of men".

A guru need not come in the sacred kavi (saffron) robes. A guru can also come in a three-piece suit, or as a very radiant, sensual, sophisticated model, or as a beggar, or as a child, or as a housewife who has no education whatsoever. So please never, ever have preconceived notions about what a guru should look like.

At the same time, beware of all those who act as gurus and make egoistic statements. Forcing people to kiss one's feet and make disciples drink water used to wash one's feet is sickening. Lord Krishna did not make his devotee Kuchela wash his feet; instead, it was Lord Krishna who washed the feet of Kuchela.

Ultimately, the one and only true guru is the inner voice within us. When we search within, we will slowly realize that we are indeed the immortal soul and not the physical body. That is the reason why Sri Aurobindo asked everyone to listen to the "inner voice".

Who is a true guru?

Bookish knowledge of the scriptures does not make someone a guru. Since guru means God himself in Hinduism, many who say they are gurus are merely teachers.

A true guru will be like a Sthita Prajna (enlightened person) as Lord Krishna described in verses 2:54–57.

Anyone who does not fit that definition is not a guru but merely a teacher.

Ultimately, the one and only the true guru is the inner voice within us. That is the reason why Sri Aurobindo asked everyone to listen to the "inner voice".

Chapter 57

What is the cosmic upside-down Asvattha tree?

Details	Verse
Lord Krishna discusses the Tree of Samsara.	15:1–3

In the fifteenth chapter of the Bhagavad Gita, the Tree of Samsara (repeated cycles of birth, death, and reincarnation) is compared to the imperishable Asvattha tree (the banyan/pipal) with its roots above and branches below in the Vedas.

The Tree of Life is a universal symbol found in many religions and cultures around the world. In various cultures, this tree is known as the Cosmic Tree, the World Tree, and the Holy Tree. Genesis (in the Holy Bible) mentions the Tree of Knowledge of Good and Evil in the Garden of Eden. According to the Bible, by eating the forbidden fruit of this tree, Adam and Eve attain original sin, and as a consequence all human beings born or yet to be born are also born with sin. In Kabbalah, the Jewish mystical tradition underlying Judaism and Christianity, two different Tree of Life symbols are used; one is upside-down and the other right-side-up. The original Tree of Life emanates out of the divine world of unity and is depicted as upside-down, with its roots flowing from the divine place of unity and infinite light.

In the Bhagavad Gita, the upside-down Asvattha tree is rooted in heaven, and its branches are the mind. This tree is nourished by the three gunas: sense objects are its buds, and the branches stretch forth to nourish the tree.

According to Lord Krishna, we have to cut down this deeply

rooted Asvattha tree with the axe of detachment. Through the image of the upside-down tree, Lord Krishna is telling us that our true home is somewhere else and we have come here just to visit. This world is only a transit lounge.

> Lord Krishna said:
> "The scriptures state that there is an imperishable Asvattha tree with its roots above and branches below and whose leaves are Vedic hymns. The one who knows all about this tree is the true knower of the Vedas."
> "The branches of this tree, sustained by the three gunas, spread above and below and have sense objects as buds. This tree also has roots going down, and these are bound to the karmic debts of the human society."
> "Since everything about this tree is very subtle, the real form of this tree is not perceptible in this world. Nobody can understand where this tree begins and where it ends, or where its foundation is. Arjuna, you have to cut down this deeply rooted Asvattha tree with the axe of detachment."
> (15:1–3)

Chapter 58

How does Lord Krishna prove to Arjuna that he is indeed everything?

After telling Arjuna that he is indeed Brahman, situated in all living entities, and that he is the beginning, the middle, and the end of all beings, Lord Krishna continued as follows:

		Verses
Among Adityas	I am Lord Vishnu.	10:21
Among lights	I am the radiant sun.	10:21
Among Maruts	I am Marici.	10:21
Among stars	I am the moon.	10:21
Among the Vedas	I am the Sama Veda.	10:22
Among Devatas	I am Devandra.	10:22
Among indriyas	I am the mind.	10:22
Among living beings	I am consciousness.	10:22
Among Rudras	I am Lord Shiva.	10:23
Among yakshas and rakshasas	I am Kubera, Lord of Wealth.	10:23
Among vasus (elements)	I am Agni (fire).	10:23
Among mountains	I am Meru.	10:23
Among priests	I am Brihaspati.	10:24
Among generals	I am Karthikeya.	10:24
Among bodies of water	I am the ocean.	10:24
Among great sages	I am Bhrigu.	10:25
Among vibrations	I am Aum.	10:25

Among sacrifices	I am Japa (chanting).	10:25
Among immovable things	I am the Himalayas.	10:25
Among trees	I am the banyan tree.	10:26
Among sages and demigods	I am Narada.	10:26
Among Gandharvas	I am Citraratha.	10:26
Among perfected beings	I am Sage Kapila.	10:26
Among horses	I am Uccaihsrava.	10:27
Among elephants	I am Airavata.	10:27
Among men	I am the monarch.	10:27
Among weapons	I am the thunderbolt.	10:28
Among cows	I am Surabhi.	10:28
Among causes for procreation	I am Kandarpa, the God of Love.	10:28
Among serpents	I am Vasuki.	10:29
Among Nagas	I am Ananta.	10:29
Among aquatics	I am Varuna.	10:29
Among departed ancestors	I am Aryama.	10:29
Among dispensers of law	I am Yama, Lord of Death.	10:29
Among Daityas	I am Prahlada.	10:30
Among subduers	I am time.	10:30
Among beasts	I am a lion.	10:30
Among birds	I am Garuda.	10:30
Among purifiers	I am wind.	10:31
Among wielders of weapons	I am Rama.	10:31
Among fishes	I am a shark.	10:31
Among flowing rivers	I am the Ganges.	10:31
Among creations	I am the beginning, middle, and end.	10:32
Among sciences	I am the spiritual science of self.	10:32
Among logicians	I am conclusive truth.	10:32

Among letters	I am the letter *A*.	10:33
Among compound words	I am the dual compound.	10:33
Among creators	I am Brahma.	10:33
Among women	I am fame, fortune, fine speech, memory, intelligence, steadfastness, and patience.	10:34
Among hymns in the Sama Veda	I am Brihat-sama.	10:35
Among poetry	I am Gayathri.	10:35
Among months	I am Margasirsa (November–December).	10:35
Among cheats	I am gambling.	10:36
Among the splendid	I am the splendour.	10:36
Among descendants of Vrishni	I am Vasudeva.	10:37
Among Pandavas	I am Arjuna.	10:37
Among sages	I am Veda Vyasa.	10:37
Among great thinkers	I am Usana.	10:37
Among those who police lawlessness	I am punishment.	10:38
Among those who seek victory	I am morality.	10:38
Among secret things	I am silence.	10:38
Among the wise	I am wisdom.	10:38

Chapter 59

What happened to Lord Krishna after the Mahabharata War?

Grandson: What happened to Lord Krishna after the Mahabharata War?

Grandfather: This is a very controversial subject, since some will emphatically say that Lord Krishna never left. It is true that Lord Krishna, as a symbol of Brahman, never left: that Lord Krishna will always live in our hearts.

But according to the Srimad Bhavata Purana and the Mahabharata itself, after the Mahabharata War, Lord Krishna left Planet Earth and went to Vaikunda, the abode of Lord Vishnu. Here is the chronology of what happened. As described in the Stri Parva of the Mahabharata, Lord Krishna took Queen Gandhari to see her 100 fallen sons on the battlefield of Kurukshethra. Seeing all the dead bodies of her beloved sons, Queen Gandhari was taken over by anger and grief and cursed Lord Krishna.

She said: "Krishna, none of this would have happened except for you. There were no reasons for my sons to die in this battle. I curse your whole family: the Yadava clan, including yourself, will die in a similar fashion."

Hearing that curse, and speaking without any anger or remorse, Lord Krishna said: "Thank you, Mother. I am eagerly looking to the day when my family is eliminated from Mother Earth."

When questioned by Sage Narada about his conversation with

Queen Gandhari, Lord Krishna reminded Sage Narada that he took form as an avatar to protect dharma and eradicate adharma. Now, having done this, his Yadava clan has become a burden for Mother Earth and must be destroyed.

In time, as Lord Krishna predicted, the Yadava clan became frivolous and hedonistic and became a burden to Mother Earth. One day all the children joined and dressed up Krishna's son Samba as a woman and met visiting Sapta Rishis. (Rishi Visvamitra, Durvasa, Vasistha, and others), who were visiting Dwaraka for an audience with Krishna.

To play a joke on the Sapta Rishis, Samba dressed as a young pregnant woman and asked the rishis to predict the gender of the baby.

The Sapta Rishis were not amused. They saw through the prank. In a fit of rage, they cursed. They said Samba would give birth to an iron bolt that would destroy his entire race.

All the Yadava kids laughed and laughed, until Samba developed labor pains. Now things became very serious. According to the curse of the Sapta Rishis, Samba delivered an iron rod.

The youth informed King Ugrasena about what had happened. He then asked Samba to grind the iron bolt into powder and cast it into the Prabhas Sea. The king also issued an order that no intoxicating spirits shall be produced or distributed in the Yadava kingdom.

Unluckily, all those iron filings were washed back to the seashore and they were somehow transformed to very strong grass. One day the Yadava clan assembled on the seashore with wives and children and they started drinking and merry-making.

They danced and used all kind of drugs. Pretty soon fights broke out among them and all of them killed one another using the grass as weapons that came from the iron filings.

Some of the powder cast in the Prabhas Sea had been

swallowed by a fish. Inside the fish, the powder had become a metal piece. Jiru, a hunter, caught that fish and found the metal.

Jiru sharpened it to make an arrow. He went hunting and accidentally shot Lord Krishna while Krishna was meditating on a tree top. Jiru thought Lord Krishna was a deer.

Seeing a bleeding Krishna, the hunter started apologizing but Lord Krishna laughed and said to the hunter:

"Please do not worry…No harm done. Believe me, I allowed you to shoot at me, since in the last life you were Bali, the monkey king and as Rama I killed you with an arrow from the side, since you were very powerful. What I did as Rama was wrong and can never be justified. So it is the karmic law that you have to kill me. That is the reason why I allowed you to kill me."

Lord Krishna also told him that he had to inform everyone in Dwaraka Palace that he had left the earth and gone back to Vaikunda. The hunter went back and informed everyone in the palace about the Swargharoon (return to Vaikunda) of Lord Krishna.

Hearing about Lord Krishna's departure, Balarama also left the body, and so too did all Lord Krishna's wives except for eight or nine. This is the way Stri Parva of the Mahabharata describes the last days of Lord Krishna on Planet Earth.

Chapter 60

What is a mantra?

Details	Verse
Lord Krishna said: "Among mantras, I am Gayatri mantra."	10:35

Grandson: Grandpa, what is a mantra?

Grandfather: The word mantra combines two root words: *man,* "to think", and *tra,* "instrument", "instrument of thought". In brief, a mantra is a magic incantation or spell. Most of the known mantras come from the Tantras. In Hinduism, all deities are represented by mantras, and each deity is associated with a particular mantra. It is said that the power of the mantra can bring down the deity to enter an image, making the image come "alive".

All Hindu mantras are made of letters of the Sanskrit alphabet. It is believed that each letter has infinite potency and that when several of these letters are properly grouped into a mantra, each letter will contribute to create a special effect.

According to the power of the mantras, they are grouped into male, female, and neutral types:

Ending of mantra	Group
hum or phat	masculine
svaha	feminine
namah	neutral

There are an endless number of mantras in Hinduism. There

are fifty-two letters in the Sanskrit alphabet, so fifty-two elements of power are available to produce many different combinations of mantras.

Of course, nobody can say that only sounds produced by the Sanskrit alphabet can become mantras. But the Hindu mantras were developed by the rishis, the ancient scientists of the Vedic age, and an in-depth evaluation of each word combination took place before the combination was accepted as a mantra.

Normally, a devotee is given a mantra by a guru, which allows the devotee to gain that mantra's full benefits. Of course, one can pick up any mantra and start chanting it, and as long as the person has faith in that mantra, he or she will receive some positive results.

Japa is the best known technique for chanting mantras. The mantra is repeated constantly, first audibly by the human vocal cords and then silently and mentally. As a devotee continues chanting his or her favorite mantra, he or she will notice changes in consciousness, but there may not be any visible change in the physical body.

There are several types of mantra, among which the Pranava and Gayatri are the most popular. The mantra Hare Krishna (ISKCON) devotees chant is:

Hare Krishna, Hare Krishna, Krishna Krishna, Hare Hare
Hare Rama, Hare Rama, Rama Rama, Hare Hare

According to the Srimad Mahabhagavatam, this mantra is specifically used to free one from Samsara or bondage .

"Om Namah Shivaya" is known as the great redeeming mantra which the Saivates (those who pray to Lord Shiva) chant. Another popular mantra is "Sree Ram, Jaya Ram, Jaya Jaya Ram." There are even mantras like the Vasikarani mantra, meant to attract the opposite sex.

Why is Japa very important?

Japa means to repeat or remember the mantra, and ajapa-japa means constant awareness. The letter *A* in front of the word japa means *without*. Thus, ajapa-japa is the practice of japa *without* the mental effort one normally needs in order to repeat the mantra.

When you chant any mantra, it will automatically make your breathing slow down, which will in the end result in controlling your thoughts. Since time immemorial, the Hindu rishis knew that breathing and thoughts were very closely connected. Thoughts reflect and affect our mood and our attitude. Thoughts are silent sounds, and sounds are electromagnetic vibrations. The more refined our thoughts, the more elevated our vibration; the more elevated our vibration, the closer we get to the highest vibration of all: our own divine nature.

Initially, you may have to use a necklace of rudraksha beads for chanting mantras, but as you become proficient, you will not need any.

What is the Gayatri mantra?

The Gayatri mantra is the most sacred mantra of the Vedas. The Gayatri mantra originates in the Hindu Rig Veda (3:62:10). Some call this mantra the Savitri mantra, since it contains the word Savitri. Legends state that this mantra was composed by Rishi Vishvamitra, who was a Kshatriya by birth and who was finally elevated to the Brahmin state because of his intense tapas and devotion.

As with any other mantra, to get the proper effects, this mantra should be accepted from a true guru. If one is going to chant this mantra, one should follow the Devanagari script. Please do not follow the English version I have given below. According to Hindu scriptures, a mantra chanted with mistakes in it is worse than chanting no mantra at all.

Personally I feel that like all other mantras, this great mantra is of Tantric origin, which may be the reason why it has unexplainable powers locked within itself. Just as the sun eradicates darkness, so does the Gayatri mantra destroy ignorance.

Recitation of the Gayatri mantra is preceded by Aum, and the Gayatri mantra reads approximately as follows:

> Aum Bhur Bhuvah svah
> Tat savitur varenyam
> Bhargo devasya dhimahi
> Dhiyo yo nah pracodayat
> (Rig Veda 3:62:10)

Which translated somewhat as follows:

"We meditate on the transcendental glory of the Creator, who is in charge of physical, astral, and causal worlds, and who pervades the universe and sustains all. May He stimulate and illuminate our minds."

Can women chant the Gayatri mantra?

There is no regulation against a woman chanting the Gayatri mantra in any of the Hindu scriptures. Those who preach that women should not chant it have no understanding of the mantra. How can a mantra which is a power source have bad effects on women? Some people say things without any scriptural backing to their statements at all.

It is true that some of the mantras in Hinduism should be chanted according to the proper yama-niyamas (dos and don'ts) in order to get the maximum benefit. But that statement applies to everybody and is not specifically against women at all.

Chapter 61

Why can't women visit some temples during menstruation?

Grandson: Grandpa, why can't women visit some temples during menstruation?

Grandfather: I know only one temple in India which forbids women from visiting the temple during menstruation. That is the Ayyappa temple in Sabarimala, Kerala.

Lord Ayyappa, the deity in Sabarimala, was born out of the union of Lord Shiva and Lord Vishnu. This temple is visited by men of all ages, but women between twelve and fifty-five years of age are prohibited from entering.

What is the scriptural thinking behind this prohibition?

One reason might be that Ayyappa was a bachelor. Still another reason, according to the temple authorities, is that women of this age group have to take care of the family while men observe the forty-one-day long ritual at the temple.

But the primary reason is that blood, in ancient times, was considered to be a part of the sacrifice to the gods. Men might have worried that women, knowingly or unknowingly, would sacrifice menstrual blood to the gods. As such, they forbade women from going to the temple during that time.

Manu Smitri addresses this issue. At the time of Manu, during menstruation, women were encouraged not to perform

288 • ED VISWANATHAN

puja or participate in most religious activities (even handling the offerings). Manu wrote in Manu Smriti: "During the four days of menstruation, a woman is infertile and unclean."

I believe Manu wrote this strictly to guard women, rather than to punish women at all. Men at those times demanded a lot from women, so he wanted women to be able to rest during menstruation: that is, stop cooking, working in the fields, doing laundry, taking care of children, and being forced to have sex by their husbands.

To me the whole restriction is a joke. If menstrual blood can desecrate a temple, how can anyone allow a pujari to conduct a puja with his fingers cut and bleeding? We have a double standard: one set of rules for men and another set of rules for women.

Today, at the dawn of the twenty-first century, many feminine hygiene products are available, and women will never drop blood on the temple grounds. Any restriction against women visiting a temple is totally unnecessary. This prohibition is not based on any scriptural ordinances or regulations at all.

Ignorance about women and ignorance about God both lead people to create crazy, sickening laws. God is God, above human emotions and human ego, and God welcomes everyone, whether clean or unclean, whether he or she is a Hindu or not. Unnecessary restrictions such as this can only make more Hindus run away from Hinduism and become Christians.

> Lord Krishna said:
> "If one offers me with love and devotion a leaf, a flower,
> fruit, or water, I will accept it."
> (9:26)

God does not care what clothes we wear or how much money we have or how much money we donate to the temple or how many baths we take before we come to the temple. The only thing God is interested in is how sincere we are in our faith. The God who ate his disciple Kuchela's beaten rice tied in a cloth and then washed his feet is above all human emotions and all human restrictions.

Religions are man-made;
Spirituality is God-made.
Religions are just ways to help a person
mature spiritually.

Ultimate goals of every human
being are spiritual maturity and
self-realization.

That meant realizing one is the
immortal soul (Atman) within the body
and giving up the false belief that one
is the perishable material body.

Who Am I?

That is one of the most thought-provoking questions a person will have in his or in her life.

Adi Sankara answered that question in his popular six-stanza prayer known as the **Atmashatkam** or **Nirvanashatkam**.

It was written around 788–820 CE.

I am not the body. I am the God within.

I am the Atman, the immortal soul, which is indeed God.

Chapter 62

What does Hinduism say about gambling?

Grandson: Did Lord Krishna say anything about gambling?

Grandfather: There is one verse (10:36) in the entire 700 verses of the Bhagavad Gita, where Lord Krishna said: "I am gambling among all deceitful practices, and of the marvellous people, I am the super. I am the victory among the victorious, the firmness of the determined, and the goodness of the good."

Even though Lord Krishna did not say much about gambling, the Pandavas' biggest problem in the Mahabharata was Yudhisthira's gambling addiction. He knew very well that Duryodhana's uncle Shakuni would cheat during the dice game, yet he still insisted on playing. He even went to the extreme extent of wagering his precious wife Panchali because of his compulsive gambling addiction.

The Mahabharata contains numerous other instances of gambling, as dice games were a source of entertainment for kings and other learned and powerful people in ancient India. Sadly, some Hindus have been hooked to the throw of the dice ever since.

Hinduism's view of gambling is conditioned by concepts of karma and reincarnation. The Hindu scriptures condemn gambling. Manu Smriti (7:50) warns people against it. In the most ascetic Hindu practices, gambling is specifically forbidden, while less stringent sects tend to look at the motivations and outcomes of gambling to determine whether or not it is moral. In general, gambling for entertainment is frowned upon.

Why is the cow important to Hindus?

Hindus do not worship cows. Hindus respect, honor, and adore cows. By honoring this gentle animal who gives more than it takes, Hindus love and care for all animals.

1.	When people settled on the banks of the Indus river and surrounding areas, the cow was the first animal they domesticated. During the Vedic age, cows were a real blessing to the community.
2.	Cows provided them with milk, butter, and yogurt. A dead cow's skin was used to make shelters and clothing. So the community in the Vedic age was really indebted to the cow in many ways. This adoration for the cow later made the community to look at the cow with devotion.
3.	The Hindu Purans talk about a celestial cow named Kamadhenu which could grant and fulfil any wish. Lord Krishna was a cowherd and he spent most of his childhood and youth taking care of cows.
4.	As time passed, the cow was looked upon as a symbol of motherhood. Even in the writings of Sage Manu, there are specific references to cows and the forbids the slaughtering of cows.
5.	To Hindus, cows are still venerated. The vast majority of Hindus still avoid consuming beef, but they do not look down upon any person who consumes beef. Anyway, among the masses in India, the slaughtering of cows will be a very controversial issue for years to come.

Chapter 63

What is the final message of the Bhagavad Gita?

Grandson: What is the final message of the Bhagavad Gita?

Grandfather: The final verse, which describes what Sanjaya said to blind King Dhritarashtra, is one of the most important verses in the Bhagavad Gita.

> Sanjaya said:
> "Wherever there is Lord Krishna, the master of all Yogas, and the archer Arjuna, there alone will be fortune, victory, well-being, and righteousness. This my opinion."
> (18:78)

What Sanjaya meant by that is "Where there are persons who are spiritual in nature and always ready to act, there alone will be fortune, victory, well-being, and righteousness." All of us should never stop acting, but we have to act in a selfless manner.

> The Bhagavad Gita is the true word of God.
> The Bhagavad Gita is the living word of God.

The Bhagavad Gita is the most thought-provoking, powerful, life-giving, and enchanting book on earth, since everything that is discussed in the Gita is universal in nature. It is the most systematic treatise available to help us deal with the problems we face in our daily lives, as well to teach us the four paths to attain self-realization.

There is no other scripture in the entire planet that can help every human being deal with their problems as well as the Bhagavad Gita, whether one is a Hindu or not.

> Lord Krishna never judged or ordered.
> He only showed to us the pros and cons of every issue and left it up to each one of us whether to follow his teachings or not.
> He did not even influence Arjuna's free will. Arjuna had the right to accept everything Lord Krishna taught, as well as the right to reject everything Lord Krishna taught.
> Throughout the Bhagavad Gita, you will not come across even one line starting with "Thou shalt not".

Can you sum up the message from the Bhagavad Gita?

Of course I can.

About duty

1) You have only the right to do your duty. You have no right to any rewards.

2) You should not act out of desire for the fruits of actions, and you should never be inactive at any time.

3) Any action done with selfish motives will only make you unhappy. So always do selfless actions (Nishkama Karma).

4) Those who have renounced the fruits of actions are released from all karmic debt and will not be born again.

5) By abstaining from action, nobody can achieve freedom from action, nor by abandonment or renunciation of all

actions can one attain perfection.

6) God has nothing to gain by action, but still acts constantly.

About sin

7) Even if you are the worst sinner in the world, you can cross over the ocean of sin with a bark of wisdom.

8) As the blazing fire burns wood to ashes, so does the fire of knowledge (jnana) burn all "karmic debt" to ashes.

About a yogi

9) A yogi lives like a lotus leaf. Raindrops fall, but the leaf is not affected by them. Similarly, a yogi lives in the world, but the yogi is unaffected by the world. So become a yogi.

About the mind

10) To those who have control over the mind, the mind is a friend; but for those who have no control over the mind, the mind acts like an enemy.

11) To one who can control the mind and attain tranquility, heat and cold, pleasure and pain, honor and dishonor are the same.

12) Whenever the mind goes unsteady and wanders, one must keep it under the control of the self.

13) The mind is restless and very difficult to control, but it can be controlled by constant practice and by detachment.

14) If you can become the master of your thoughts, you can become the master of your life as well the master of the world around you.

15) When a person constantly thinks about objects, attachment for those objects arises in the mind. From attachment, desire is born, and from desire, anger is born. From anger comes delusion; from delusion comes loss of memory. From loss of memory comes destruction of

the intellect, and once the intellect is destroyed, a person perishes.

Birth and death

16) Death is certain for anyone who is born, and birth is certain for anyone who dies. Therefore, there is no reason to lament over the things that are inevitable.

17) All beings are not discernible before birth and after death, only between birth and death. Therefore, there is no cause for grief.

18) After many births and deaths, the person who has the full knowledge of the self (Atman) surrenders to God, knowing that God is everything.

The immortal soul

19) The soul (Atman) within the body is unborn and eternal. Atman is not slain when the body is slain.

20) No one can destroy the imperishable Atman.

21) Just as a person puts on new garments after giving up old ones, similarly, Atman secures new bodies after giving up old bodies.

Creation and annihilation of the universe

22) By God's will, the whole universe is created and annihilated again and again.

23) A day of Lord Brahma, the God of Creation, lasts for a Kalpa, and his night lasts for another Kalpa. Again and again, when Brahma's day arrives, all living entities come into being, and with the arrival of Brahma's night, they are helplessly annihilated.

24) One Lord Brahma, God of Creation, lives for 311.04 trillion human years. After that another Brahma will appear.

About salvation

25) Salvation is for everyone. Nobody is denied salvation.

26) The best among us attain salvation after one life; the worst will only attain salvation after many lives.

27) You do not have to be a Hindu to attain salvation.

28) Hindu salvation is the process by which a person realizes that he or she is not the perishable body but the Atman, the immortal soul within the body. That is the reason why Hindu salvation is known as self-realization.

29) Lord Krishna said there are four paths to attain salvation. They are:

Jnana Yoga	Path of knowledge
Karma Yoga	Path of selfless actions
Raja Yoga	Path of breath control and pranayama
Bhakti Yoga	Path of devotion

Lord Krishna never judges or orders throughout the Bhagavad Gita.

He only shows to us the pros and cons of every issue, leaving it to each of us to decide whether or not to follow his teachings.

He did not even influence Arjuna's free will. Arjuna had the **right to accept** everything Lord Krishna taught, as well as the **right to reject** everything Lord Krishna taught. In fact, at the end of the Mahabharata, Rishi Veda Vyasa has to come and teach a broken-hearted Arjuna the Bhagavad Gita all over again.

Throughout the Bhagavad Gita, you will not find even one verse starting with "Thou Shalt Not".